WALKS AROUND MALMESBURY

& NORTH WILTSHIRE

Judy Jones

Blue Tree Books

First published in 2008 by
Blue Tree Books, 28 Back Hill,
Malmesbury, Wiltshire,
SN16 9BT, United Kingdom

Revised edition published in 2010
Text and images copyright © Judy Jones 2008, 2010

A catalogue record for this book is available from the British Library.

ISBN 978-0-9557682-2-4

Printed and bound in the United Kingdom by
CPI Antony Rowe, Chippenham, Wiltshire

Pubs update:
Since publication the **Saladin,** Little Somerford (p.93)
has become the **Somerford Arms; the Bell,** Broad Hinton
(p.153) is now the **Barbury Inn**; the **Rose & Crown,**
Brokenborough (p.183) has been renamed the **Horse
Guards** and the **Suffolk Arms,** Brinkworth (p.169) has closed.

CONTENTS

Author's Foreword and Acknowledgements

Welcome to the revised edition of this book which goes to press after one of the coldest dampest winters in living memory. Through the grim weeks of January and February, as we slithered from icy paths and frost-bitten country lanes to the mud baths created by the thaw, signs of the coming spring around Malmesbury were, quite literally, thin on the ground. However, friends and I found much to lift our spirits during the short country walks we took in near-zero temperatures early in 2010: spotting an egret bathing in the river at Brokenborough, huge numbers of fieldfares hopping around a pasture by the Thames at Ewen, and a close encounter with a polecat scampering across Goose Bridge in Malmesbury, bold as brass, spring to mind. The chance to see wildlife and get some fresh air and exercise are reasons enough to go walking – but what else makes the countryside around Malmesbury and North Wiltshire worth exploring on foot?

To me, it's the sheer variety of landscape within a relatively small area, and the vast network of public rights of way that enable us to see it, that make this part of the world special. Here we can see the humble beginnings of two mighty rivers – the Thames, near Kemble and the Wiltshire Avon (also known as the Bristol Avon) around Tetbury and Sherston, near Malmesbury; explore the south of England's very own lake district – the Cotswold Water Park; walk the towpaths alongside disused canals around Cerney Wick, near Cricklade, Lacock, south of

Chippenham and Sapperton, east of Cirencester; discover the awesome sights and changing colours at Westonbirt Arboretum; and sample the fabulous panoramic views from the iron age hill fort Barbury Castle, south west of Swindon and from Box Hill across the By Brook valley towards Bath. Sprawling south from the heart of the Cotswolds to the northern outcrops of the Wiltshire Downs, are also quiet stretches of farming country and parkland that often appear little changed over the centuries.

The 25 routes featured in this guide mostly lie within North Wiltshire. Malmesbury is only a couple of miles from the county boundary with Gloucestershire, and so a few of the routes are over the border. All but one of the routes (Ewen) appeared in the first edition and have of course been re-walked and re-checked to ensure that the step-by-step directions are as clear, accurate and up to date as possible. I have made some minor changes to the routes of four walks – Corston, Brokenborough, Long Newnton and Box Hill – mainly to try to add interest. In the case of Corston, it was to include a great bridleway that was cleared and re-opened in 2008 as part of a programme of path improvements around Malmesbury by Wiltshire Council. I hope readers will get as much enjoyment out of using this book – all year round – as I've had researching it.

I am grateful to the route testers whose helpful input is reflected in the final text: Sue Alexander, Bill and Julie

Cavendish, Doreen Chandler, Steve and Hilary Cox, Ginny Parfitt, Glyn and Linda Davies, Mike Elam, Vanessa Fortnam-King, Marion Farrelly and Paul Mewton, Sharon Nolan, Carolyn and Ian Kennedy, Anna Palmer, Trish Pollard, and Lesley Saunders. Thanks to Alison Griffiths for the author photo, also to the landowners, council officers, Ramblers and others who work to maintain the vast network of public rights of way around Malmesbury and North Wiltshire.

Market Cross and St Paul's bell tower, Malmesbury

About This Guide

The walks range in length from 3 to 8 miles and are designed to appeal to a broad range of walkers, from beginners upwards. Each walk is given a star-rating to indicate the level of physical challenge it presents:

*   Easy
**   Moderate
***   More challenging

Points of historical, cultural and architectural interest are highlighted along the way, as are the pubs. The title illustration across pages xii and xiii shows the broad geographical area that provides the focus of this book and the walk names and numbers.

Sketch maps

The numbers you see on the sketch maps correspond to the step numbers that start each section of the route text. Although not essential, you might want to take the relevant OS map to help you get the most out of the walk. Most of the 25 routes described are within the area covered by OS Explorer 168: Stroud, Tetbury and Malmesbury. The rest are within OS Explorer 156: Chippenham and Bradford on Avon, 157: Marlborough or 169: Cirencester & Swindon.

Walking safely and responsibly

The better you prepare for walking, and anticipate potential problems, the more you will get out of the experience. Ensure that you are properly clothed and equipped, check the weather forecast before setting out, and be aware of your legal responsibilities, as well as your rights.

You might consider taking:
- Backpack
- Mobile phone
- Water
- Map and plastic map holder
- Binoculars/camera
- Small notebook/pen or mini-tape recorder
- Waterproof jacket/trousers
- Proper walking boots, with ankle support, (or good quality, comfortable wellies) and thick socks
- Snack – fruit and/or chocolate bar
- Money
- Secateurs
- Skin protection/sun block and a wide-brimmed hat

Follow the Countryside Code
- * Keep to the public rights of way and permissive paths
- * Leave gates and property as you find them
- * Protect wildlife, and take litter home
- * Keep dogs under close control, and pick up after them
- * Be considerate of others

On occasions, you may walk along short sections of roads without pavements. Unless you see a good reason not to, remember to face the oncoming traffic when walking along roads, so that you and any drivers approaching you can see each other.

Dogs

Keep dogs under close control at all times, and on a lead when near livestock. Guidance from the Ramblers and the National Farmers' Union in 2009 however, advises that if you feel threatened by cattle, let the dog go as the cattle are most likely to chase the dog, not you. Walk around the herd if you feel at risk and re-join the footpath when safe to do so.

Footpath problems?

If you come across obstacles or other problems on a public right of way, please do report these to the relevant highways authority or to the Ramblers (ramblers.org.uk) who are happy to pass on to the relevant council reports they receive, as appropriate. For the purposes of continuing your walk, you are entitled to find an alternative way around an obstruction on a public right of way, if you are unable to remove it.

Public transport

Five of the walks described start and finish at the Market Cross in Malmesbury – Lea, Corston, Little Somerford, Malmesbury Circular Walk and Brokenborough. The Long Newnton and Westonbirt walks start and finish in Tetbury. For details of bus services operating in the area, ask at Tourist Information Centres, or phone Traveline on 0871 200 22 33 (travelinesw.com). Railway stations serving the area covered by the routes in this book are at Kemble, Chippenham and Swindon.

Parking in Malmesbury:

Malmesbury lies off the A429 Chippenham to Cirencester road, 5 miles north of Junction 17 of the M4. The long stay car park is at the old station yard, off Gloucester Road, Malmesbury. Here's how you get there.

Coming north from Chippenham and the M4 – Junction 17: Travelling north on the A429 go straight on at the roundabout just past Malmesbury's new health centre and stay on the by-pass over the second roundabout by the water tower and a garage. Take the next turning left along Filands, and the next left after that towards the town centre. At the double mini-roundabout at the bottom of the hill, near a supermarket, turn left to the pay-and-display long stay car park.

Coming south from Cirencester and the M5:
Travelling south on the A429 from Cirencester, pass a garden centre on your left as you approach Malmesbury, go all the way round the roundabout by the water tower and back the way you came. Take the first turning left along Filands – opposite the garden centre – and the next left. Continue to the double mini-roundabout near a supermarket and turn left there to reach the long stay car park.

From this car park head towards the Abbey and turn right over the river along Mill Lane. Walk up the Abbey steps. Brass plates on the steps feature some of the key events in the town's history.

Follow the path between Abbey House Gardens (left) and the Cloister gardens (right) to emerge by the Market Cross. To visit Malmesbury Tourist Information Office (tel. 01666-823748) go left here along Oxford Street, then first right into Market Lane, then left again into Cross Hayes: the office is then on your left in the Town Hall.

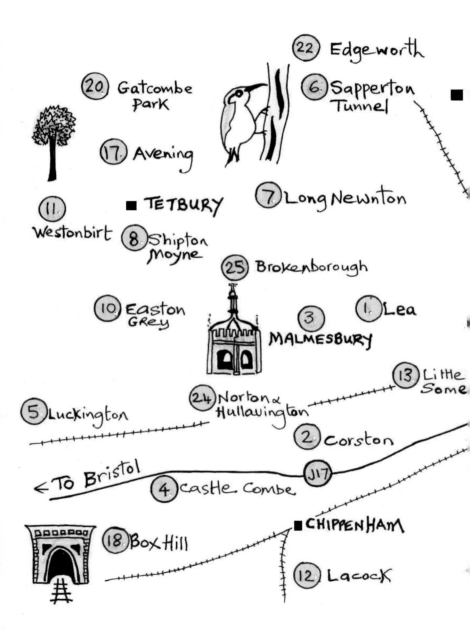

(22) Edgeworth

(20) Gatcombe Park

(6) Sapperton Tunnel

(17) Avening

(7) Long Newnton

(11) Westonbirt

■ TETBURY

(8) Shipton Moyne

(25) Brokenborough

(10) Easton Grey

(1) Lea

(3) MALMESBURY

(13) Little Some

(5) Luckington

(24) Norton & Hullavington

(2) Corston

<To Bristol

(4) Castle Combe

J17

■ CHIPPENHAM

(18) Box Hill

(12) Lacock

WALKS AROUND MALMESBURY AND NORTH WILTSHIRE

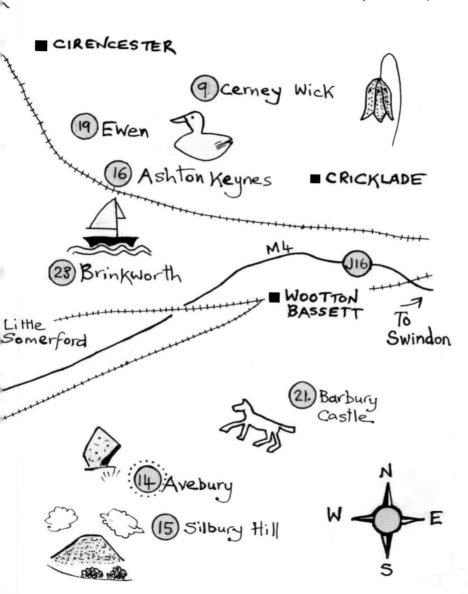

■ CIRENCESTER

⑨ Cerney Wick

⑲ Ewen

⑯ Ashton Keynes

■ CRICKLADE

㉓ Brinkworth

M4

Ⓙ16

■ WOOTTON BASSETT

To Swindon

Little Somerford

㉑ Barbury Castle

⑭ Avebury

⑮ Silbury Hill

N

W   E

S

1. LEA

Distance:	3½ miles
Time:	1¾ hours
Pub:	Rose & Crown, Lea
Map:	OS Explorer 168: Stroud, Tetbury & Malmesbury
Star-rating:	* Easy
Start/End:	Market Cross, Malmesbury ST 934873

A short walk over farmland from Malmesbury to the village of Lea via Milbourne and back over Cowbridge Weir. The Rose & Crown at Lea has a pleasant, good-sized garden next to the churchyard and plenty of room inside.

Route:

From the Market Cross, Malmesbury take the lane running alongside the Whole Hog and the footpath to the left of the entrance to Abbey House. Go down the Abbey steps over the river bridge and straight on to reach the **Conygre Mead (A)** nature reserve on your right. Turn right into the mead and follow the river path, from which you can glimpse through the fence part of **Abbey House Gardens (B)**, soon to meet a road junction.

1. Turn left and almost immediately right up to Blicks Hill. You can either walk along the lane or take the footpath left through trees which runs alongside it.

Cross the main road (A429) with care and go straight on through a wooden gate to walk along a lane with hedges on each side.

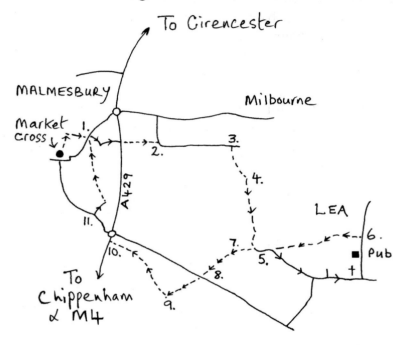

2. On reaching a road junction, turn right (in effect, you are continuing in the same direction) and pass a red telephone box. Use the grass verge on the right where necessary.

3. Continue straight on across the entrance to Monks Park, take the next turning right onto a narrow lane, passing some new houses on your left. The lane soon becomes a track that leads to a large field.

4. The right of way goes diagonally right over the top of the field, but many people walk along the field edge on your right, and then turn left at the bottom corner near a metal gate. Follow the bottom edge of the field up to a stile on your right, just before a track leading to a farmhouse. Go over the stile and down the hill, bearing slightly left, towards a wooden gate near the river and a narrow lane. Once through the gate turn right onto the lane to pass Crab Mill.

5. Keep going to the end of Crab Mill Lane, then turn left and go straight on across the entrance to Pembroke Green. Follow the road as it bends left around St Giles Church. You soon reach the Rose & Crown pub (tel. 01666-824344) on your left. Continue in the same direction for about 150 yards.

6. Take the next turning left into Rushcroft Close. Go over a stile at the end of a path into a field. Bear diagonally right across the field to pass through a gate, and then go straight down the hill, keeping a hedge on your left, to meet a brook. Turn left through a gateway and then turn right towards a pair of stiles that lead you back to the lower end of Crab Mill Lane. Turn right onto the lane and, as it bends right up towards farm buildings, pass through the wooden gate (on your left) that you came through earlier.

7. Keeping the brook on your left, proceed along the lower edge of the field to a stile into another field. Aim for a gap in the old railway embankment ahead – once part of the **Malmesbury branch line (C)** and continue through it to a bridge over the Avon at Cowbridge Weir.

8. Follow the lane to the main road, passing the former site of **Cowbridge House (D)** on your right. Cross the main road (B4042) and pick up the footpath opposite via a stile into a field. Follow the river along the bottom field edge past some World War II defences then up to the top corner.

9. Turn sharp right and follow the top field edge to reach a stile into the next field. Cross this and bear diagonally left up the hill, passing a small fenced area of young trees on your left, to pass over a stile at the brow of the hill. Follow the path downhill, aiming to the right of the new health and care home complex ahead. Pass through a wide wooden gate set in the fence ahead of you into the next field. Go diagonally right across the field and over a stile in the corner. Go straight on keeping a boundary on your right over one last stile onto a track leading to a main road (A429).

View towards Malmesbury from hillside east of Lea

Birds on the brook near Crab Mill

10. Cross the road by the zebra crossing and bear right along the pavement down through Burton Hill and Parliament Row towards the Town Bridge, Malmesbury. Turn left onto the footbridge (just before the road bridge) then turn right through the Memorial Gates. On reaching the pavement, note the plaque on each gate depicting the old borough seal of Malmesbury and, on the opposite side of the road, at the junction with St John Street, a medieval hospital that later became almshouses. Turn left and walk a few paces to a bend in the road.

Snowfall on Back Hill and Goose Bridge

11. Cross the road and continue ahead into St John Street. Go over the narrow road bridge (Goose Bridge) and keep going alongside the bowls club. Take the footpath left running alongside the far edge

of the bowls club, so that you pass behind the score board. Stay on the path through two fields to reach Holloway Bridge. Cross the road, with care, and pick up the river path opposite. Follow the river path back through Conygre Mead, then retrace your steps back to the Market Cross.

Notes:

A: **Conygre Mead** is a Local Nature Reserve, providing habitats for hundreds of species of flora and fauna. The mead is owned by the Malmesbury River Valleys Trust, established in 1992 as a place for wildlife and quiet recreation. Visit mrvt.org.uk for more information.

B: Ian and Barbara Pollard, also known as the Naked Gardeners, have transformed the five-acre **Abbey House Gardens** into a riot of spring, summer and autumn colour – and an international tourist attraction. The gardens are open to the public from March to October. Visit abbeyhousegardens.co.uk for more information about opening times and special events.

C: **The Malmesbury branch line** operated passenger rail services from Dauntsey (on the London to Bristol main line) between 1877 and 1933 and from Little Somerford between 1933 and 1951. Freight continued on this GWR branch railway until its final closure in 1962. The station yard is now mostly occupied by Malmesbury's long stay car park. The history of the line is told in Mike Fenton's *The Malmesbury Branch.*

D: **Cowbridge House,** demolished in 2007 to make way for the new housing development you see now, was thought to date back to the late 1700s. Built for the Brooke family of Brooke Bond Tea fame, it was later the home of Baldemiro de Bertodano, who in 1902 co-founded the St Aldhelm's Freemasons' Lodge in Malmesbury. Bob Browning's book *Ecko's of Cowbridge* tells the story of the house and the "war factory" that developed RADAR on the site.

2. CORSTON

Distance:	6 miles
Time:	3 hours
Pub:	Radnor Arms, Corston
Map:	OS Explorer 168: Stroud, Tetbury & Malmesbury
Star-rating:	** Moderate
Start/End:	Market Cross, Malmesbury ST 934873

Spectacular views of Malmesbury open up as you cross sloping farmland south west of the town en route to Corston, and its charming pond. You pass the north eastern edge of King's Heath, held by the commoners of Malmesbury for more than 1,000 years. You return along one of the many bridleways in the area that were cleared and re-opened at the end of 2008 after years of overgrowth had made them impenetrable. Mainly level.

Route:

Facing the top of the high street with the Market Cross behind you, turn right along Gloucester Street. At the first corner go straight on under the mirror along an alleyway downhill. Go down the steps, turn right onto a metalled path and on joining a road go left across the entrance to a housing estate and join the path going between two stone walls. Follow the path over the river Avon (Sherston branch) past a weir and into the water meadows.

Walk 2: Corston

Cross a stream via an old stone footbridge, known as a clapper bridge, at **Daniel's Well (A)**.

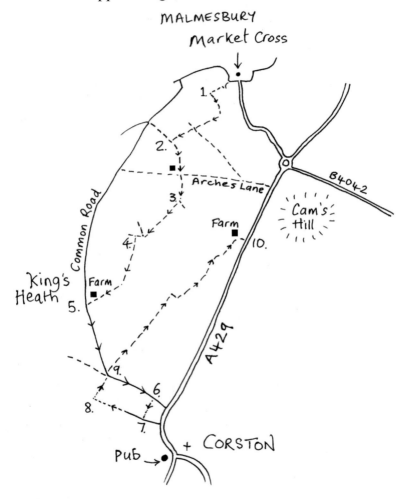

10

1. Turn left to pass through a gap between a stone wall and a hedge. Continue straight on keeping the hedge on your left and then cross into the next field via a kissing gate. Turn right and follow the path slightly uphill and keep a field edge on your right. Pass a derelict stone building then turn right to cross the stile ahead of you into the next field. Go diagonally left across the field uphill, keeping a boundary on your left, and cross into a fourth field via a stile at the top left corner near a large oak tree. Continue straight ahead on the path to exit the field via a stile next to a wide gate.

View towards Malmesbury from top of Arches Lane

2. Turn left onto a byway and pass a converted barn and a farmhouse on your right to reach a junction of tracks. Go straight on to join a metalled lane and keep going in the same direction, past fields on either side, for about 400 yards.

3. Follow the lane as it bends right and then, about 10 yards after it starts bending left, towards another converted barn, turn right through a wide gap in the hedge and a gateway into a large sloping field. Follow the path along the left hand field edge uphill, round a corner and then as it turns left and left again. At the next corner, turn right past a gate and keep going slightly uphill (still with a hedge on your left) to the top left corner of the field. Go through a gateway to reach a junction of paths. Go straight on along a bridleway soon to walk with hedges on either side of the path.

4. About 200 yards after the junction cross the stile on your left into a sloping field. Go straight down the hill aiming for the bottom right corner of the field near an electricity pole. Once you've reached the corner, go through a walker's gap next to a wide metal gate and turn left to go through a pair of gates (or open gateways) separated by a footbridge across a ditch into the next field. Turn right cutting across the corner of the field and pass through a gap in the hedge and tree line into the next field to see farm buildings straight ahead of you. Bear slightly left across the field towards the gate to the right of a large tree. Go through the gate and straight across the next field towards an electricity pole to the left of the farm buildings. Go over the stile set in a fence

ahead of you and continue past the electricity pole to reach a pair of stiles separated by a footbridge. Once over these, continue in the same direction, keeping a hedge on your right, over another two stiles to reach Common Road. Ahead of you is **King's Heath (B).**

5. Turn left along Common Road. After about ½ mile, shortly before the brow of a slope and a bend in the road, you reach a bridleway on your left. If you need to shorten your walk and miss out the Corston section, turn left along this bridleway to return to Malmesbury and continue from step 9 on page 14. Otherwise keep going along Common Road past a byway junction, a footpath and later three bungalows all on your right.

Corston pond and nature reserve

6. Turn right onto a bridleway just past the third bungalow, soon to see **Corston village pond (C)** and an information board on your left. Continue to the end of the bridleway and a T-junction.

7. Here you have a choice: to visit the Radnor Arms (tel. 01666-823389) at the centre of Corston, turn left onto Mill Lane and follow this to a T-junction with the A429 Chippenham to Cirencester road. Turn right along the pavement. The pub is then about 100 yards on your right. Retrace your steps back to this junction and up Mill Lane. If not visiting the pub turn right off the bridleway along Mill Lane. At the top of the lane, pass West Park House and go through a gateway into a large area of open space, with a wood away to your left. Pass a line of trees and a private drive on your right.

8. Immediately after the private drive, go through a gate on your right and follow the path over a stile into a field. Keep a hedge on your right as you pass to the other side of the field and a stile onto Common Road. Turn left and continue along Common Road as it bends right past the byway junction mentioned at step 5. Keep going on the road for about 20 yards to reach a bridleway on your right.

9. Turn right off Common Road onto the bridleway flanked by hedgerows on either side. In winter, there are far-reaching views left and right through

the branches as the bridleway follows a ridge. Over to your right, for example, you may be able to see a landmark familiar to many in this area the **Rodbourne water tower**, built in 1957; and later **Cam's Hill**. To the left are more views over King's Heath and the farmland you walked across earlier. After about ¾ mile the bridleway bends right, then left and slightly uphill. You pass some gates on each side and gently descend towards farm buildings. Go through a gate onto a farmyard and bear right along a short lane to reach a T-junction with the A429.

View from bridleway on the way back to Malmesbury

10.   Turn left onto a pavement adjoining the main road, which was turnpiked in 1755-56, evidence of which can soon be seen as you pass on your left Pike

House with its distinctive bay front. Continue for about ½ mile.

11. After passing 30 mph signs on the outskirts of Malmesbury, take the next road left Arches Lane. Follow this downhill passing the entrances to Burton Hill caravan park and to Orchard Court. At the bottom of the hill, take the footpath signposted right via a stile in a stone wall. Keep a field boundary on your right and pass a gate as the path bends left uphill. Go over the stile just beyond the top of the hill. Continue downhill for a few yards and take the stile on your right you cross earlier on the outward leg of the walk. Retrace your steps to the Market Cross.

Notes:

A: **Daniel's Well** is thought to be named after a 7th or early 8th century monk. According to the medieval historian William of Malmesbury, Daniel would frequently immerse himself in a spring here in order to purify his spirit.

B: **King's Heath** was granted to the burgesses of Malmesbury by King Athelstan, grandson of King Alfred, after the town's menfolk helped him defeat the Danes at the Battle of Brunanburh in 937 AD. The 600-acre stretch of almost prairie-like farm land is still held by their descendents. The Warden and Freemen of Malmesbury, or the Old Corporation, which also owns many properties in the town.

C: **Corston Pond,** an important habitat for toads, was created in the 1950s out of the deepest part of an old limestone quarry. The wildflowers that grow around it from April to September include scabious, oxeye daisies and orchids. The first Local Nature Reserve to be so designated in North Wiltshire, this peaceful and pleasant spot is owned by the Malmesbury St Paul Without Parish Council and maintained by villagers.

3. MALMESBURY CIRCULAR WALK

Distance:	3 miles
Time:	1¾ hours
Pub:	The Smoking Dog, Malmesbury High Street
Map:	OS Explorer 168: Stroud, Tetbury & Malmesbury
Star-rating:	* Easy
Start/End:	Market Cross, Malmesbury ST 934873

This gentle stroll around the rural fringes of Malmesbury, via Milbourne, brings fine views of this historic hill-top town's distinctive skyline and architecture, dominated by the Abbey. You also see some of the town's splendid buildings, gardens and rivers. The Abbey and the Abbey House Gardens are well worth exploring.

Route:

From the Market Cross, cross the road and walk down the High Street. Half way down turn left into St Dennis Road, then right into Silver Street and then down Back Hill.

1. At the foot of Back Hill steps turn left into Baskerville, go over Goose Bridge and pass the bowls club. Continue under the by-pass and over a cattle grid along the metalled drive through a field. Here you are walking parallel with the route of the **Malmesbury branch railway line (A)** on your left.

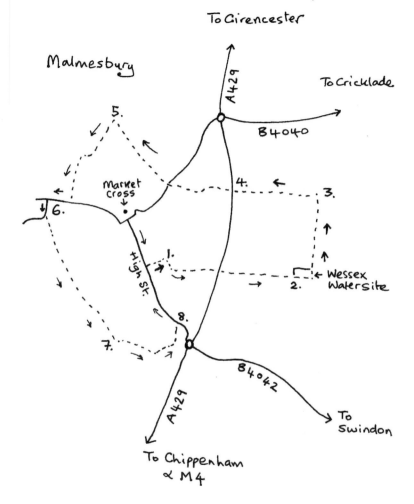

2. At the end of the drive go over the stile next to the Wessex Water site entrance. Follow the path

through the trees and after passing through a gate at the end, turn left uphill. Keep a hedge on your left. At the corner of the field turn left onto a track, go over a stile onto a track and follow this track until it meets a road.

3. Turn left onto the road. Soon you bear left by a phone box onto a no through road. Once through the wooden gate at the end, cross the main road (A429).

4. Continue ahead along Blicks Hill. To avoid walking on the steeply descending road, you can take the footpath to your right - once used by alighting passengers of horse-drawn carriages to lighten the load. Watch out for a wooden kissing gate (near the entrance to a large house) leading onto the footpath.

Frosty morning, Conygre Mead

At the T-junction at the foot of the hill, cross the road with care and join the path opposite between a car park and the river. Once through the wooden gate into Conygre Mead turn right following a path uphill. At the junction of paths at the top, turn right then left across the cricket ground car park. Go over a stile and then follow the footpath along the left edge of the ground behind the club pavilion. After another stile, continue downhill. Straight ahead you may see the distinctive undulating roofline of the Dyson building surrounded by tall trees; and to the right the Reeds Farm housing development.

5.   At the foot of the hill, exit the field via a kissing gate and turn left. Follow the pavement on the left side of the main road past the supermarket and bus stop over the river bridge. Continue uphill past the mini-roundabout. After about 100 yards, cross the road and walk up the first turning on the right Foundry Road. At the top turn left past some terraced cottages, shortly emerging onto Horsefair. Bear diagonally right across Horsefair then go left along West Street. At the next road junction, turn right onto Bristol Street. On your immediate right you can see a cottage that began life as **St Helen's Church**, believed to date back to the 10th century.

6.   Where Bristol Street bends round to the right, turn left down Foxley Road and go over Truckle Bridge. From the bridge and just beyond it, there are fine views up to the crescent-shaped south western edge

of the of town centre, including the Old Bell Hotel, the Abbey and the bell tower and spire of St. Paul. After passing the river, bear left up a narrow lane past a stile on your left. After passing barns on your right, go through a metal gate ahead of you across the yard, and then over a stile next to another gate. Walk straight on keeping an old hedge on the left, towards a stone building next to a gateway. Go through the gateway and continue in the same direction uphill towards a stile next to a metal gate. Go over the stile and continue in the same direction keeping a hedge on your left. Go past a gate as the path bends right to meet a stile in the bottom corner of the field onto Arches Lane.

7.   Turn left onto the lane. Over to the right you will soon see the grounds of what used to be **Burton Hill House (B)**. Go past the entrance to Orchard Court on your left and at the next junction, a few yards further on, take the alleyway with metal bars on each side. At a junction of paths, turn right and stay on it through a housing estate. At the end of this, turn left past a red post box into Parliament Row and continue downhill on the pavement.

8.   Take the footbridge, left, over the river and go right through the Memorial Gates to reach a pavement. Turn left up the High Street, which shortly bends round to your right. You soon see the Smoking Dog pub (tel. 01666-825823) on your right. Carry on up the High Street back to the Market Cross and bear

left through Malmesbury Abbey (C) grounds and past the Old Bell Hotel. Note the brass footplates sunk into the pavement just before Mill Lane, marking the site of the old West Gate. The inscription quotes the poet **John Betjeman (D)** on the "sacred atmosphere" of Malmesbury. Across the road there are lovely views across the river valley towards Arches Farm and beyond. Return to the Market Cross via the Abbey grounds or Birdcage Walk near the mirror.

Plaque showing Malmesbury's historic borough seal, Memorial Gates

Notes:

A: **Malmesbury branch railway line**: See the notes accompanying Walk 1 Lea.

B: **Burton Hill House** was re-built in the early 1840s. Colonel Charles Miles, who promoted the building of a branch railway to Malmesbury and served on the Malmesbury Railway Company board, owned the property for many years. From 1936-1945, the house was leased out as a private school. After World War II, the house was sold to the Shaftesbury Society for use as a school for disabled children. This closed in 2007.

C: **Malmesbury Abbey,** and town, owes their origins to a Celtic Monk called Maildulph who in 642 set up a hermitage on top of the hill. The Abbey was founded in 675 by Aldhelm, whose canonisation and shrine attracted pilgrims to the town. Malmesbury was much favoured by Saxon kings, as a source of good loyal fighting men ready to take on the Danes. The 14th century stone effigy of King Athelstan lies in the Abbey. Famous for its cloth, silk and wool, Malmesbury also became known in the 17th and 18th centuries as one of the most corrupt of "Rotten Boroughs".

D: In the early 1960s, **John Betjeman** made a short film about Malmesbury in a series of 12 on the West Country towns he loved. Three decades later Gerry Dawson, an HTV producer, unearthed the films. As a result the films have been re-released on video as *The Lost Betjemans.*

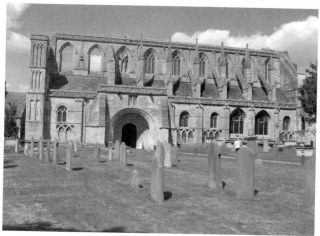

Malmesbury Abbey

4. CASTLE COMBE

Distance:	5 miles
Time:	2½ hours
Pubs:	White Hart Inn, Ford
Map:	OS Explorer 156: Chippenham
Star-rating:	** Moderate
Start/End:	Visitors' car park, Castle Combe ST 846777

An enchanting walk through a wooded valley, past clear rushing rivers and streams, and finally into Castle Combe, once voted the most beautiful village in England. The White Hart Inn at Ford and St Andrew's Church are well worth a visit. There are a couple of gently sloping inclines. Starts and finishes at Castle Combe – about 10 miles south west of Malmesbury (about 20 minutes drive).

Route:

From the visitors' car park just north of Castle Combe, walk down the steps to the road, turn right and at the road junction right again towards the village. Continue for about 100 yards.

1. Fork right onto the footpath signposted to Nettleton Shrub via School Lane and go past some houses. Pass between two concrete posts to skirt the left edge of the golf course, keeping a metal fence, and then a stone wall, on your left. Stay close to the wall

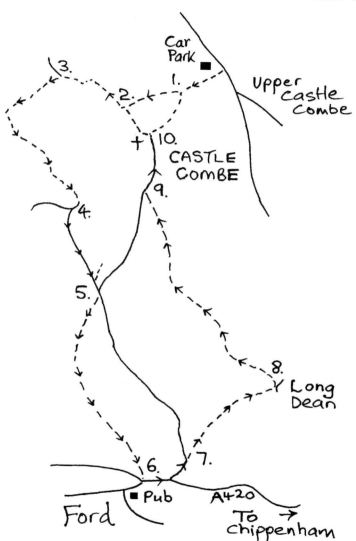

Car Park

Upper Castle Combe

1.

2.

3.

10.

CASTLE COMBE

9.

4.

5.

8.

Long Dean

7.

6.

Pub

Ford

A420

To Chippenham

as the path descends through woods. Ignore the footpath striking off left into the village. A few yards beyond it are good views of the church tower and stone roofs of **Castle Combe (A)**. You soon emerge from woodland onto the Manor House golf course.

Frost on the fairway, Manor House Golf Course

2. Continue along the path to join the metalled drive, turn right and then go left over the stone river bridge. Continue through the golf course and just before another bridge take the path on your left into woodland, keeping the brook on your right. Continue to a metal gate set in a stone surround.

3. After walking a few yards turn left between two houses. At the end of this path turn left and cross the

river via a stone bridge and continue uphill to a road junction.

4.   Turn left onto a minor road and continue for about ½ mile, with a wooded area falling away steeply to your right. (**Note**: if you need to curtail your walk, there is a **short cut** you can take back to Castle Combe. After passing a sign on your left to Shrub Farm, take the next footpath and descend through woods down to a road. Turn left on reaching the road and walk back into the village.) To complete the full version of the walk, continue straight ahead on the minor road.

5.   Just after the next road junction, fork right via a wide metal gate onto a footpath through mixed woodland and then along a hillside down to a brook. Once over a stone stile and a footbridge, bear left into a field and follow the path towards the village of Ford.

6.   On reaching the main road (the A420) cross the road with care to visit the 16th century White Hart (tel. 01249-782213), which is signposted. It serves morning coffee and afternoon teas as well as lunches. Otherwise turn left on reaching the main road along the pavement by the road, and take the first road left signposted Castle Combe. (If you visit the pub, retrace your steps to the main road and turn right, then take the first road on your left uphill

towards Castle Combe.) After about 250 yards of walking uphill, the road begins to level out.

7. Go over a stile to your right and take the path cutting across the top left side of the hill ahead of you, then down through woods into the hamlet of Long Dean.

8. At the junction of narrow lanes and footpaths, with a red post box ahead, bear left. Stay on this wooded path, part of the **Macmillan Way (B),** until you reach the southern edge of Castle Combe. The path rises gently uphill and then down, with a river on your left.

9. After crossing the stone river bridge, turn right towards the village (past public toilets on your left) along a road. As you proceed through the village note **St. Andrew's Church (C)**, set back from the road, on your left just before the road junction.

10. You have a choice of routes back to the car park. **a)** Turn right, between the two pubs, uphill to return via the **Castle Combe Museum (D)**. Take the next left after the museum back up to the car park. **b)** To avoid much of the road-walking, and the museum, go straight past the turning to the church, keeping the Castle Inn on your right. Follow the road uphill, behind the Manor House Hotel entrance, and continue along the footpath underneath a stone arch. After crossing the stile at the top of the steps, turn right. Here you are back on the same path,

bordering the golf course, where your walk began. Retrace your steps to the visitors' car park.

Cobbled lane, Castle Combe

Notes:

A: **Castle Combe** was transformed into a fictional fishing port for the filming of *Dr Dolittle* (1967), and voted the most beautiful village in England a year later. The 14th century Manor House, is now a hotel, with a much admired golf course. The Castle Combe motor racing circuit, formerly a World War II airfield, lies about a mile north east.

B: The main route of the **Macmillan Way** long-distance coast to coast path (running from Boston, Lincolnshire to Abbotsbury, Dorset) was established to promote and raise funds for Macmillan Cancer Relief.

C: The **parish church of St Andrew,** dating back to the 13th century, contains some stunning stained glass; and an unusual monument to a Norman knight, Walter de Dunstanville, a great-great-grandson of Henry I of England, who lies in stony, chain-mailed repose with his legs crossed. This posture suggests he fought in two crusades, according to Leonard Lack's short history of the church. Don't miss the glass-encased faceless clock, one of England's earliest timepieces.

D: **Castle Combe Museum** contains a wealth of fascinating old photographs, maps and other artefacts, and opens on Sunday afternoons from Easter to October.

5. LUCKINGTON

Distance:	4 miles
Time:	2 hours
Pubs:	Old Royal Ship, Luckington;
	Rattlebone Inn, Sherston
Map:	OS Explorer: 168: Stroud, Tetbury &
	Malmesbury
Star-rating:	* Easy
Start/End:	Sherston High Street ST 853858

A relaxing and mainly level stroll from the attractive ancient hilltop village of Sherston south west to Luckington. You go through woodland, across farmland, and past the grounds of Luckington Court, featured in the acclaimed BBC TV adaptation of Jane Austen's Pride and Prejudice in 1995. Sherston lies 5 miles west of Malmesbury – about 10 minutes drive – on the B4040. Parking is available in the High Street. Bus service 41 runs between Malmesbury and Sherston, Monday to Saturday.

Route:

Walk along the High Street, **Sherston (A)** away from the church and the Rattlebone Inn (tel. 01666-840786), bearing left behind a stand-alone building (the doctors' surgery) and then down a dip. Take care on the short section lacking a pavement.

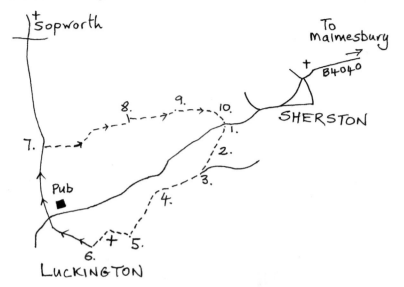

1. Just after crossing the river Avon, take the footpath signed left over a stone stile into a field. At the bottom of the grassy steps bear right and walk along the field edge keeping a post and rail fence, and a river on your left. Nearly half way down the field, cross the river footbridge and then go right through a wooden kissing gate and follow the path as it winds between trees. The river is now on your right. Soon the path leaves the woodland and takes you into a field.

2. Continue ahead along the path which shortly turns left uphill near a telegraph pole. Where the land begins to flatten out, bear right towards the top

corner of the field. Cross over the stone stile into the next field. Bear left across the field and then exit it at the bottom left corner through a gap to reach a lane.

3. Turn right onto this lane. As you approach houses, take the footpath to the right of the ford.

4. At the end of the ford, turn left at the crossroads onto a signposted no through road, continuing through the attractive hamlet of Brook End. On meeting water again, take the footpath to the right of the river.

Luckington lion – near St Mary &
St Ethelbert Church

5. On reaching a large Cotswold stone house on the right, you see a stone wall ahead of you. Turn right here up towards the church. Just before the entrance to the farm complex, go left through a small wooden gate to walk along a path round the back of the church. As you head for the wooden gate out of the churchyard onto the green, you may see part of **Luckington Court (B)** on your right. As you walk through the green you may see the spire of Alderton church to your left. On reaching the end of the green, pass through the gate and cross the road.

6. Turn right and walk along the pavement past the entrance to **Luckington Court**, on your right. Pass a children's recreation ground on the left and head towards the telephone box. Before crossing the main road to join the Sopworth road ahead, note a splendid example, on your right, of a "tin tabernacle" – Luckington Methodist Church. You will see the **Old Royal Ship (C)** almost immediately on your right on the other side of the main road (B4040). Continue ahead along the Sopworth Road. Follow this quiet minor road for about ½ mile until reaching a track on the right (signposted byway) near the top of an incline.

7. Turn right onto the track and stay on this for nearly a mile.

Tin tabernacle – Methodist church at Luckington

8. At a T-junction of tracks opposite a wide metal gate, turn left. Continue for about 50 yards, and then go over the low wooden fence on your right into a large field. Pass to the right of the remains of hedge ahead of you then follow the path across the middle of the field to reach a wide gate set in a hedgerow at the bottom of a slope. Go through the gate in the hedgerow and keep going with a hedge and then a stone wall on your right.

9. When the wall ends, walk towards the top right corner of the field, and pass through a metal gate. Keep to the right side of the next field. At the edge of a plateau go straight ahead, and down the hill to cross a stone footbridge over the river.

10. Turn right to return to the main road, then go left up the hill to return to the centre of Sherston.

Notes:

A: Artefacts unearthed in and around **Sherston**, including the remains of a villa, and its proximity to the Fosse Way, suggest a strategic importance in Roman Britain. The unusually wide high street of this former borough boasts several fine 16th century buildings. Sherston hosts its annual Boules Festival, said to be the largest outside France, in July.

Boules festival, Sherston

B: **Luckington Court** was transformed into the fictional country house of Longbourn in Andrew Davies' memorable BBC TV adaptation, broadcast in 1995 of Jane Austen's *Pride and Prejudice*. The marriage scene was filmed next door – in the Church of St Mary and St Ethelbert, founded by the Abbot of Malmesbury, in 1265 AD. Sir Winston Churchill's "Spymaster", Major-General Sir Stewart Menzies (1890-1968), head of the Secret Intelligence Service during World War II, lived at Bridges Court, Luckington for most of his life. Known as "C" to his colleagues, Sir Stewart is said to have inspired the fictional intelligence chief "M" in Ian Fleming's James Bond spy thrillers.

C: The **Old Royal Ship** at Luckington (tel. 01666-840222) came to the rescue when the supplier of hot lunches to the village primary school pulled out. Since June 2001, the pub has provided the children's meals.

6. SAPPERTON TUNNEL

Distance:	3 miles
Time:	1¾ hours
Pub:	Tunnel House Inn, Coates
Map:	OS Explorer 168: Stroud, Tetbury & Malmesbury
Star-rating:	* Easy
Start/End:	Near Coates Village Hall SO 978007

Visit the source of the Thames, and walk along an old canal towpath to reach the Coates entrance of the famous Sapperton Tunnel. The Tunnel House is a super pub, with plenty of space to sit outside. This level well-signposted walk starts and ends in Coates, 11 miles (15-20 minutes' drive) north of Malmesbury off the A433 Cirencester-Tetbury road. On street parking available near Coates village hall.

Route:

Keep Coates village hall and the recycling site on your right as you walk to the end of the road. Go left at the T-junction, signposted Kemble and Tetbury. Cross the road to walk on the grass verge.

1. After about 250 yards, take the stone stile on the right onto a footpath leading away from the road. Continue alongside the field edge, keeping a stone wall on your right. Go over another stone stile at the

far right hand corner of the field, and bear left
downhill, with a stone wall now on your left.

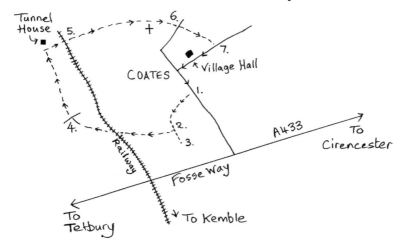

2. After passing some farm buildings on your left, and
once over an old canal bridge, you reach a junction
of footpaths. Go straight on here, and soon over a
stepped stile to the left of a gate, then shortly
another. Keep the woodland on your left as you
approach a third stile.

3. Once over this walk about 100 yards shadowing the
left hand field boundary to reach a simple
commemorative stone marking the **source of the
Thames (A).** Retrace your steps back to the
signposted junction of paths by the old canal bridge.
Turn left here onto the path adjoining the old
Thames and Severn Canal (B), which is part of the

Monarch's Way, soon to pass underneath a railway bridge (Kemble to Stroud line). Look out for a derelict **round house (C)** on your left.

*Round house between
Coates and Tarlton*

Tunnel House sign

4.   Where the path forks, take the lower path under a road bridge. As you approach road level, you soon see the eastern (Coates) entrance – of the **Sapperton Tunnel (D)**. Go up some steps to emerge opposite the Tunnel House Inn (tel. 01285-770280). Turn right to walk over the tunnel mouth, and then as the drive bends right, go left over a wooden stile into a small sloping field.

5.   Walk uphill through the field and go through the gate ahead. Take great care as you cross the railway line and pick up the path leading into a field. Go straight across the field and pass through a gap in

the stone wall ahead into the next field. Continue along a grassy path heading diagonally right across the field, soon joining a track that passes to the left of farm buildings. On a clear day, away to your right, the Wiltshire Downs and Kemble church spire are visible on the skyline. On reaching a road, go straight on past Coates church on your right soon to reach a T-junction.

View towards Coates church from the west

6.   Cross the road, and pass through a wooden gate opposite. Keep going with trees on your right. Pass through a wooden kissing gate and go straight on in the same direction, keeping a hedge on the right, towards a metal gate and a road.

7. Turn right onto the pavement, passing cottages built for Bathurst estate workers, soon to find Coates village hall again on your right.

Notes:

A: **Source of the Thames:** Barely legible now, the inscription on the commemorative stone reads: "The Conservators of the River Thames 1857-1974. This stone was placed here to mark the source of the river Thames". A few feet in front of the stone lies a hollow where, after heavy rainfall, you may be able to see a few bubbles and the odd puddle. While a few sceptics insist the *real* source of the river is about 11 miles north of here at Seven Springs, near Andoversford, this spot – known as Thames Head – is generally accepted as correct.

B: The **Thames and Severn Canal** was completed in 1789 to link the Stroudwater Navigation with the Thames at Lechlade. The Cotswold Canals Trust (cotswoldcanals.com) is working to restore these waterways to navigation after decades of disuse. A similar operation is under way to open up the North Wilts Canal. The plan is to link the two canals once again at their original junction at Latton, between Cricklade and Cerney Wick.

C: This **round house** was originally a lengthman's home. There were five such homes along this 37-mile long canal, and the lengthmen – as the name suggests – looked after their particular lengths of it.

These canal company employees carried out maintenance, cut back vegetation, dealt with any leaks and generally watched out for trouble. In the case of the Thames and Severn, each employee would monitor just over 7 miles of canal, living roughly midway along their stretch. Typically, there was shelter for livestock on the ground floor, living accommodation above, and a cone-like structure at the top for collecting rainwater for drinking.

D: Extending just over 2 miles, the **Sapperton Tunnel** was once Britain's longest canal tunnel. Boats would have been "legged" through the tunnel – there being no path inside for hauling them through.

7. LONG NEWNTON

Distance:	3 miles
Time:	1½ hours
Pub:	Snooty Fox Hotel, Tetbury
Map:	OS Explorer 168: Stroud, Tetbury & Malmesbury
Star-rating:	* Easy
Start/End:	Long stay car park, old rail yard Tetbury ST 893934

Look out for red kites and buzzards above the tree tops around Preston Park on this mainly level walk from Tetbury to Long Newnton church. A pleasant tree-lined path laid on the route of the former Tetbury branch railway takes you past one of the two sources of the Bristol Avon. Tetbury lies about 5 miles north west of Malmesbury along the B4014. To reach the long stay car park, turn right at the first mini-roundabout by the Snooty Fox. Continue along the Chipping past the short stay car park and take the next right to the old railway yard.

Route:

From the long stay car park and with the ex-railway goods shed behind you take the path heading away from the centre of Tetbury, keeping steep limestone banks on your right. Pass picnic benches on your left, and beyond them a river bed – often dry.

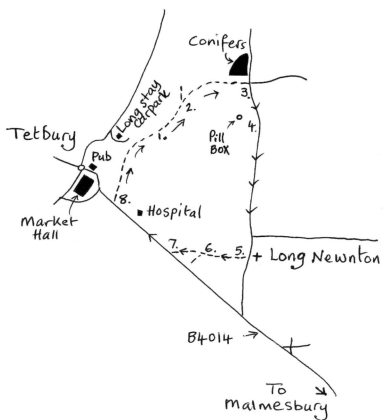

1. Keep going past a wooden footbridge on your left, signposted Herd Lane, and soon you see a large sloping open space beyond the river bed which is **Preston Park (A)**, and a small stone footbridge. A little further on along the disused **Tetbury branch railway (B)** you see another stone footbridge on

47

your left near Wor Well – one of the two sources of the Bristol Avon (the other is near Sherston, west of Malmesbury).

Rail path, Tetbury

2. Just before a gate in front of you go right along a path uphill (sometimes very muddy) for about 20 yards to pass through a wooden gate. Bear left and follow the path around the side of a hill, passing a large pool of water and an electricity pole on the left. Continue ahead, keeping the boundary of a large farmhouse on your right, soon to join a track. Follow the track as it bends right and goes over a cattle grid. The track then gives onto a metalled lane, taking you past a conifer wood on your left. Keep going up the lane to a crossroads at the brow of the hill.

3. Turn right at the crossroads, signposted Long Newnton and Crudwell, along a quiet country road with a grass verge on the right and far reaching views on each side. Away to your right, the spire of Tetbury church can be seen, and a few miles beyond it the radio mast at Goose Green (off the Tetbury to Wotton-Under-Edge road near Newark Park), a familiar landmark for miles around. Further on you pass on your right a pill box, one of the many defences built to protect Bristol during World War II.

Holy Trinity Church, Long Newnton

4. When the road starts to bend right, panoramic views start to open up towards the beech clumps on the Wiltshire Downs and the Ridgeway, ahead and left (including Liddington Hill, south east of Swindon,

on the far left horizon, and Cherhill Down, south east of Calne, on the centre left horizon). Follow the road as it bends left and pass a pair of 40 mph road signs and a left turn signposted Crudwell. Continue to the entrance gates of **Long Newnton Church (C)** on your left.

5. Turn right onto a wide bridleway opposite the church entrance gates and keep a hedge on the left and a stone wall on the right.

6. When the bridleway bends left, go straight ahead on a footpath via a wooden gate into a field. Keep a field boundary on your right, as you continue downhill. At the bottom end of the field, go through a gap to meet the B4014 Malmesbury-Tetbury road.

7. Cross the road with care and turn right onto a pavement back towards Tetbury, passing the entrances to the Great Tythe Barn and to the hospital both on the right. Just after the hospital entrance, cross the road to join the pavement on the hospital side.

8. Just before meeting the bridge at the bottom of the hill (Wiltshire Bridge) turn right through a wooden gate onto a footpath signposted Tetbury Rail Yard. Follow this path back to the long stay car park. To reach the Snooty Fox (tel. 01666-502436) and other pubs and cafes in Tetbury take the signposted footpath, just before the car park, to the Town Centre via Gumstool Hill.

Notes:

A: **Preston Park** was originally known as the old Herd as it was part of the drovers' route to Tetbury Common on the north western outskirts of the town. It was re-named in 1955 when the land was given to the Feoffees (Lords of the Manor), whose origins date back to the early 1600s and who still maintain it as an open space for people to enjoy.

B: **The Tetbury branch** was a 7½ miles long single track railway connecting Tetbury with the Great Western Golden Valley line at Kemble, with intermediate halts at the Trouble House, Culkerton, Church's Hill, Jackaments Bridge and Rodmarton. It operated from 1889 to 1963. Trouble House halt is thought to be the only station in England to have been built specifically to serve a pub. The landlord provided customers with a beer crate to step up to, and alight from, the trains.

C: The unusual blue sundial on the south face of **Holy Trinity Church** tower is well worth a look.

8. SHIPTON MOYNE

Distance:	4 miles
Time:	2 hours
Pub:	Cat & Custard Pot Inn, Shipton Moyne
Map:	OS Explorer 168: Stroud, Tetbury & Malmesbury
Star-rating:	* Easy
Start/End:	Shipton Moyne Village Hall ST 891896

What connects the first English novel with the Estcourt family, landowners around Shipton Moyne for seven centuries? Find out on this gentle ramble, mainly level, through pasture and parkland, and along an attractive river valley. There are fine views towards Tetbury church and on the return leg, the distinctive church tower at Shipton Moyne, which lies 3 miles north west of Malmesbury off the B4040 Sherston-Malmesbury road. Once out of Malmesbury take the second turning on the right. Parking is often available in The Street, Shipton Moyne.

Route:

Take the waymarked footpath opposite Church Lane, and the village hall in the centre of Shipton Moyne. Walk between two low stone walls, and then go over a stile into a field, and soon over another stile into a second field. Go straight across this field, and over a third stile to reach a fourth one in the hedge ahead. Continue ahead in the same direction on a wide grass path through a plantation.

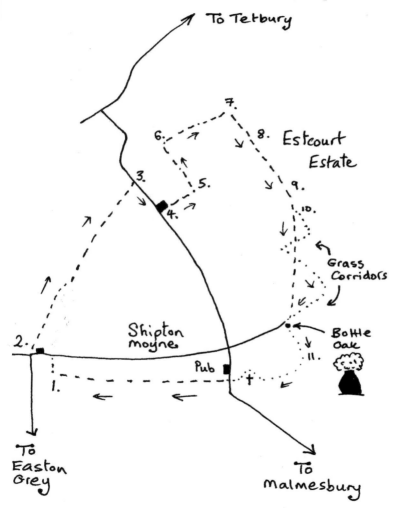

Walk 8: Shipton Moyne

1. Follow the path to the corner of the field, and then turn right following the field edge towards a road. Keep a hedge on your left. Go through a wooden gate next to a stable on your left and turn left onto a lane.

2. After about 150 yards, turn right onto a bridleway next to a stone house called Crossroads. The bridleway can be rather boggy in wet weather. There are good views across the valley on your left about half way down the track. Ignore the footpath striking off left towards Doughton and Highgrove. At the end of the bridleway, cross the road.

3. Turn right to walk along a grass verge towards a pair of semi-detached cottages.

4. Turn left onto a footpath running past the cottages. Go through a wooden gate and soon you should see the spire of Tetbury church in the distance to your left.

5. After passing an old barn, go left through a wide metal gate onto a grassy walkway, and proceed downhill towards a river valley. Go through a stile by a gate and continue down towards a brook and a wooden footbridge. Go over the footbridge.

6. Turn right keeping the brook (sometimes dry) on your right and continue along the floor of the valley through this field and a second larger field. After passing through a line of trees crossing the second

field, continue in the same direction to go through a wide wooden gate ahead. Follow the path for about 100 yards, and then turn right slightly uphill to go through a small wooden gate by a large tree.

7.   Turn immediately right, and go over the stile, onto a grassy path, with a fence and hedges on the right. After about 50 yards, go through a gate on the right and then down some steps towards the river and a stone footbridge. Then go over a wooden footbridge and a stile into the parkland of the **Estcourt Estate (A)**.

Over the stream, Estcourt Estate

8.   Walk uphill keeping a plantation (Thorn Covert) on your right, towards the first in a series of white posts marking the right of way through the estate. Bear right just before reaching the metalled drive

and walk alongside the drive, still keeping the plantation on your right, until you reach a wide wooden gate and a smaller gate next to it.

9. Go through the smaller gate and follow the drive past estate buildings and an old walled garden on your left. After the last house on your right, turn right and soon go over a stile towards fields. (The right of way goes across the fields at an angle. However, to avoid the livestock, walkers are invited to use the grass "corridors" separating the fields.)

10. Go left along a grass corridor here and then on reaching a junction of these walkways, turn right. Soon, go over a stone stile on your left, and turn right. Follow the corridor round to the left, until you meet a second junction of walkways. Turn right at the junction. About 100 yards before a wooden gate directly ahead of you, pass through a small wooden gate to the left and continue along the path until you reach a metalled drive. (Detour right here to see an ancient and unusual tree by walking a few yards to a bend in the road. On your right is what's known locally as the "bottle oak".)

11. Turn left along the metalled drive, keeping a hedge and fence on your left. About 30 yards before the entrance to a large house turn right onto path through trees and go through a small wooden gate. Turn left then right towards a wide gate and adjoining stile. Cross over the stile to enter a large field. Aim towards **Shipton Moyne (B)** and its church tower with a single turret. Note the double domed roof (left) of **Hodges Barn (C)**. Take the wooden stile (the left one of two close together) out of the field and continue towards the church. Pass through a metal kissing gate ahead and follow the path around the right side of the church. Pass through the church gates to emerge onto a lane, soon to meet a T-junction with The Street by the village hall. Opposite is the Cat & Custard Pot Inn (tel. 01666-880249).

Inn sign, Shipton Moyne

Notes:

A: The **Estcourt** family lived here from the early 1300s, later ascending to Gloucestershire's landed gentry. In the early 18th century, when England was at war with Spain, **Thomas Estcourt** financed a famous sea expedition to the eastern Pacific to capture Spanish gold. Mariner Alexander Selkirk only survived this violent, scurvy-ridden escapade after being marooned alone for four years on the island of Juan Fernandez - an experience which inspired Daniel Defoe to write *Robinson Crusoe* published in 1719, later hailed as England's first novel. In 1996 the estate passed out of the Estcourt family's ownership: "It's tragic," Desmond Estcourt told *The Times*. "But what's the good of whining? The fact is that I have run out of money." The estate is now a stud owned by Prince Khalid Abdulla's Juddmonte Farms.

St John the Baptist Church, Shipton Moyne

B: **Shipton Moyne** appears in the Domesday Book as *sciepton*, meaning "sheep town". The village church features memorials to various Estcourts and to another prominent local family, the Hodges. Formerly known as the Estcourt Arms, the Cat & Custard Pot's current name dates back at least to 1931. It is thought to derive from a reference in R.S. Surtees' book *Handley Cross or Mr Jorrocks's Hunt*, first published in 1854.

C: **Hodges Barn** is a 15th century dovecot converted into a family home, with a six-acre garden – open on certain summer days. Please phone 01666-880202 for details.

9. CERNEY WICK

Distance:	6 miles
Time:	3 hours
Pub:	The Crown Inn, Cerney Wick
Map:	OS Explorer 169: Cirencester & Swindon
Star-rating:	** Moderate
Start/End:	Cricklade Town Hall car park SU 100934

A treat of a walk for all seasons on level ground alongside the Thames and then two linked former canals undergoing restoration. You pass through North Meadow near Cricklade where thousands of snakeshead fritillaries create a spectacular display from late April into May. The walk starts and ends in Cricklade – 11 miles east of Malmesbury, a 20-minute drive along the B4040.

Route:

From the car park next to Cricklade Town Hall, cross the road and turn right along the High Street pavement passing the splendid Jubilee Clock – on your right by a road junction.

1. Just before the River Thames, turn left along North Wall. After about 30 yards, bear right to join the Thames path, and enter a field. Keep a boundary on your left as you aim for a metal kissing gate across a gap in the tree line ahead in front of houses.

2. Once through the gap, bear right past houses on your left, go through a metal kissing gate on the right, and head left across the field. Continue through a metal gate onto a path.

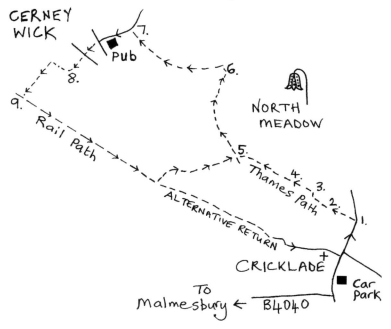

3. Once level with a large barn, turn right over a small footbridge, signposted Thames Path. Follow the path round the back of the barn.

4. Go through a metal gate on your left and continue on the path, keeping the river on your left. You soon enter **North Meadow (A)**. Stay close to the Thames until you reach a footbridge over the river. Don't cross the bridge. Go over the stile to the right of the bridge, and then turn sharp right, keeping the river behind you.

Snakeshead fritillaries, North Meadow, salute the spring

5. Continue straight ahead along the path, keeping a field boundary on your right (and North Meadow beyond it). As you enter a copse you soon see part of the old **North Wilts Canal (B)** on your left. Carry on over a footbridge until you reach a fence enclosing the grounds of a house. Go right just before the fence, following the path over a wooden footbridge. Continue ahead onto a drive, going over a cattle grid, then a bridge.

6. About 10 yards after the bridge, turn left and go over a stile next to a metal gate to your left. Go

straight on following a track for about 50 yards, to an information board. Follow the path as it bends right down a slope towards the main road (A419) soon to bend left. Keep a metal fence and a tree line on your left. Now you have the route of the former **Thames and Severn** canal on your right. On reaching a road, you should see ahead a restored round house or lengthman's cottage built to house canal workers in the 18th century.

7. Turn left onto the road, soon to reach the **Crown Inn** (tel. 01793-750369) and a T-junction. Continue in the same direction across the road and go over the stile next to a signpost. Keep going soon to cross over a narrow lane, and pick up the path again straight ahead of you. Go through a pair of metal kissing gates. Take the stile to your right into another field, and follow the path with a hedge on your left and a sailing lake – part of the **Cotswold Water Park** – on your right.

8. Follow the path as it bends right, and soon left. After about 100 yards, exit this lakeside area by taking the footpath on your left, down some wooden steps over a footbridge into a field. Keep going on the path and exit the field via a stile to join a bridleway – once part of the **Midland & South Western Junction Railway (C).**

*Fly takes a break on the canal path east of
Cerney Wick*

*Bridge over the railway path, on the way back
to Cricklade*

9. Turn left onto the bridleway and keep going until you go through a wooden gate across the track. Here you have a choice of routes back to **Cricklade (D).** You can go left to re-join the Thames Path, and after the footbridge over the river (mentioned at point 4), return the way you came via North Meadow. Otherwise, continue along the old railway track to the outskirts of the town, then follow the National Cycle Network route 45 signs, past St Sampson's Church, back to the High Street. Turn right to return to the car park.

Notes:

A: **North Meadow,** a 112-acre National Nature Reserve managed by English Nature since 1973, has the UK's largest wild population of snakeshead fritillaries. These delicate wildflowers bloom towards the end of April or early May. One of England's few remaining ancient Lammas meadows, unimproved and never ploughed, this large sweep of lowland attracts a host of invertebrates, and aquatic birds.

B: The **North Wilts Canal** opened in 1819 to connect two pre-existing canals – the Wilts and Berks and the Thames and Severn. All three canals are undergoing restoration. Look out for the information boards just past the house.

C: **The Midland & South Western Junction Railway**, built in the late 1800s, linked Cheltenham with Andover in Hampshire. Towns along the route included Cirencester, Cricklade and Swindon. Enthusiasts have restored one section of the defunct line to create the Swindon and Cricklade Railway, on which steam trains run regularly.

D: Founded by King Alfred to help defend the kingdom of Wessex from marauding Danes, **Cricklade** is the most northerly town in Wiltshire, as well as the first town on the Thames. The river was navigable here until the early 19th century. Tourist information is available at Cricklade Town Council, 113 High Street, Cricklade (tel. 01793-751394).

10. EASTON GREY

Distance:	5 miles
Time:	2½ hours
Pub:	Cat & Custard Pot, Shipton Moyne
Map:	OS Explorer Stroud, Tetbury & Malmesbury 168
Star-rating:	** Moderate
Start/End:	Shipton Moyne Village Hall ST891896

An uplifting walk through varied landscape along part of the ancient Fosse Way and past the site of a Roman settlement. Mainly level, the route features farmland, river crossings and a charming Cotswold village mentioned in the Domesday Book. Shipton Moyne lies about 3 miles north west of Malmesbury, off the B4040 Sherston road. To schedule a pub stop about two-thirds of the way round, you may want to park off-road at the junction of the B4040 and the Fosse Way, and start/finish the walk at that point in step 4 below.

Route:

From the centre of Shipton Moyne, go along Church Lane opposite the Cat and Custard Pot (tel. 01666-880249) and walk through the church gates. Bear left around the side of the church and follow the path to the metal kissing gate at the end of the churchyard.

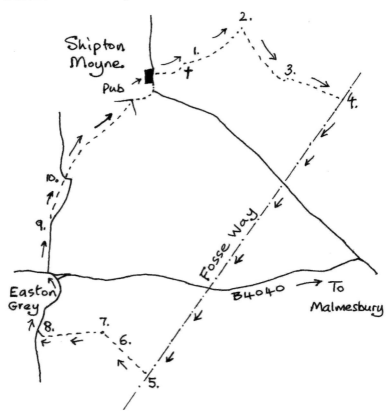

1. Go though the gate onto a grassy path with trees on each side. Continue over the stile near a sundial into a field. Follow the path across the field, bearing left of the mature trees in the middle of the field. Cross the stile to the right of a gate, continue ahead to a second gate and turn left soon to pass through a smaller gate on your right. Follow the path past trees on your left, go across a drive, then aim for a metal gate at the far right hand corner. Pass through the gate onto a grassy walkway and go straight on until you reach a farmhouse on the left.

Heading east from Shipton Moyne through
morning mist

2.   Look out for a path going off to the right just beyond a gap in the hedge. Take this path and walk downhill between post and rail fences. At the bottom of the hill*, bear left through a narrow wooden gate to walk diagonally uphill aiming for the top far left hand corner of the field and a line of trees. Exit this fenced field via a wooden gate and cross a metalled drive. Head for the stile slightly to your left into a plantation of young trees. (*If there are animals in the field, you can turn left at the bottom of the hill and walk along a grassed track to

reach a metalled drive. Turn right onto the drive and walk uphill to meet a line of trees on the left at the top. Take the stile on your left into a plantation of young trees.)

3. Once over this stile bear diagonally right onto the mown path, across a wide gap between the trees, to reach a pair of stiles at the far side of the plantation. Go over these. Bear slightly left across the field to reach a stile in the hedge ahead of you.

4. Once over this, turn right to join the **Fosse Way (A)** and continue on it for about 2 miles. You cross a minor road and later the B4040 Malmesbury to Sherston road. After crossing this second road, the Fosse Way runs close to the eastern edge of what was once a World War II Italian Prisoners of War camp, known as **Easton Grey Camp (B)**. As you descend towards the River Avon (Sherston branch) note the field on your right – once the Roman settlement of **White Walls (C)**.

5. Immediately after crossing the stone bridge, turn right off the Fosse Way via a wooden stile and continue uphill along the footpath. Approaching the top of the hill, go over a wooden stile at the side of a gate. Keep the hedge on your right all the way to the next stile, and then walk down to a wide gate. Continue downhill and bear left, over the river via a footbridge near a weir.

6. Bear right along a well-defined path uphill through woodland. Emerge into a field, go straight on keeping a hedge on your left. After about 150 yards, pass a gap to reach the corner of the field.

7. Turn left through another gap into the next field and follow the path diagonally across the middle of it. Ahead, and slightly to the right, **Easton Grey House (D)**, set in parkland may be visible, and, further right, the tall chimneys of the lodge house near the church. Climb over the wooden stile ahead into a smaller field, and follow the path down towards farm buildings passing through a gate to reach a road. Follow this road round to the right, downhill and emerge into the village at a road junction near a river bridge, thought to date back to the 16th century.

8. Turn right and walk uphill through the village, then onto the pavement on the left. Once past the entrance to the lodge house, there is a second set of gates going left leading to **Easton Grey Parish Church (E)**. At the junction with the main road, turn left opposite the bus shelter and almost immediately right across the road to join a lane signposted Shipton Moyne.

9. Once past Church Farm, the lane soon bends to the right. Take the waymarked footpath to the left here through a metal gate and bear right. Head towards a telegraph pole and the spire of Tetbury church. Exit the field before reaching the pole via another metal gate on your right.

10. Cross the road, and the stile in the hedge opposite. Follow the path through this field alongside a line of telegraph poles, aiming for a stile in the fence ahead. Once over this continue in the same direction until you pass the last but one telegraph pole. Go left here (between the last two telegraph poles) and then bear diagonally right to exit the field via a stile in a hedge to reach a road junction. Continue straight ahead, keeping fields and beyond it the church tower on your left into Shipton Moyne.

Notes:

A: **The Fosse Way** stretches from Exeter to Lincoln and the section you walk along here forms part of the county boundary between Wiltshire (left) and Gloucestershire (right). The Romans built this the first arterial road in Britain to link the Midlands and the West Country. On a clear day you should find good views to your left towards Malmesbury and the northern foothills of the Wiltshire Downs and the Ridgeway.

B: The observation tower of the WWII **Italian Prisoners of War camp** is visible from the Fosse Way. The inmates painted ornate floral designs onto the walls and ceiling of one particular hut, which they used as their chapel.

C: Excavations of **White Walls** near this spot have yielded several Roman ornaments and coins, jewellery and roof tiles. The settlement serviced and supplied passing traders and imperial messengers between the first and fourth centuries A.D.

D: **Easton Grey House:** A manor on this site was mentioned in the Domesday Book as under the ownership of Roger de Berchelai (later anglicised as *de Berkeley*). Occupants became closely connected, by marriage, with the Hodges family of Shipton Moyne. In the early 20th century, the house was used by the Duke of Windsor (when still the Prince of Wales) as a hunting base; and by Lord Asquith, prime minister from 1908-1916, as a summer holiday retreat. In the 1950s and 1960s, the house hosted a fashion business Peter Saunders Tweeds, relocated from Scotland to Wiltshire. The current 18th century house and gardens were open to the public for many years. Peter Saunders wrote a book *Almost A Fairy Story*, describing the history of the house and his family's connection with it.

E: No known dedication exists for the **Parish Church of Easton Grey.** Its rectors from 1311-1937 are listed to the left of the entrance. The tower dates back to the 15th century; the rest of the church was rebuilt in 1836.

Bridge over the Avon at Easton Grey

Easton Grey, looking north from the river

11. WESTONBIRT

Distance:	7½ miles
Time:	4 hours
Pub:	Jack Hare's Bar, Hare & Hounds Hotel, Westonbirt
Map:	OS Explorer 168: Stroud, Tetbury & Malmesbury
Star-rating:	*** More challenging
Start/End:	West Street long stay car park, Tetbury ST 930888

Lovely parkland, undulating fields, woods, and valleys provide a dream of a walk. You pass the northern fringes of the Highgrove estate, and the extravagant Victorian mansion built by the creator of Westonbirt Arboretum. An optional extension, through the arboretum itself, adds another 2½ miles to the distance above. Starts and finishes at Tetbury, a 10-minute drive (5 miles) north west of Malmesbury. Long stay parking (free on Sundays) and public toilets are at West Street near Tetbury church and Tourist Information Centre (tel. 01666-503552).

Route:

Walk along West Street away from Tetbury church, past Prince of Wales Row, slightly downhill. At the next road junction, turn left downhill along a pavement. Take the footbridge over the stream (sometimes dry) and continue along the road for about 200 yards past houses on each side.

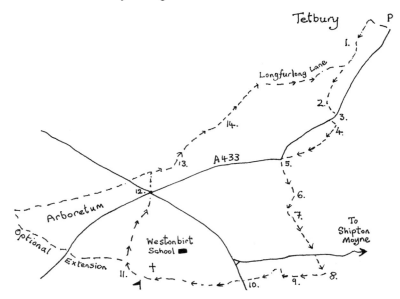

1. After a pair of 30 mph signs, go right into Longfurlong Lane. Just after the lane bends right, take the footpath left over a stone stile. Walking parallel with a stone wall away to the left, follow the path towards a dip and a line of trees ahead. Go over another stile and a wooden footbridge into a field and continue straight ahead, keeping a stone wall and then a hedge on the left.

2. Just before reaching a small stone store, turn left through a gap between a hedge and the building, then go immediately right, keeping a stone wall on your right. At the corner of the field, go over a wooden stile and then footbridge to join a road.

Footbridge south of Tetbury

3. Turn right onto the pavement and follow it for about 100 yards. Cross the road (A433) with care and take the minor road, signposted Shipton Moyne, which runs alongside Close Nursery.

4. Opposite the nursery entrance take the stone stile right over a wall into a field. Head for the far left hand corner of the field, in a dip, keeping the near clump of trees on your left. At the corner, go left through a gap in the hedge and then turn immediately right onto a track. Continue straight ahead, keeping a ditch and a hedge on your right. At the end of this field continue ahead through an open

77

gateway, keeping a post and rail fence on your left. You soon come level with the rear boundary wall of **Doughton Manor,** which dates back to the 15th century. Go straight on through the farmyard to join a metalled road.

5. Before meeting the main road, turn left by a noticeboard and left again past a new house on your right via a track and then go straight ahead, bearing slightly left, on a footpath through a field towards a line of trees. Continue towards a gap in the hedge, go through it then over a footbridge and across a track. Keep going ahead through the next field with a hedge and trees on your right.

6. Go over a stone stile into another field. Walk diagonally right across the field gently downhill. Go through an opening at the far right corner, just before a wide wooden gate near a brook (sometimes dry). Turn left and then cross a stone bridge right next to a stone wall. Continue uphill, keeping the mossy stone wall on your right, to reach a wooden gate.

7. Go through the gate and, after a few paces, turn right at a crossroads of paths, onto a bridleway, and continue walking with trees on each side. On reaching a road junction, go straight over the road and straight on along a lane signposted Easton Grey.

8. Just after a cluster of houses you reach the entrance to farm buildings, on your right. Here, take the

footpath indicated right into a field via a stile. Go straight across the field keeping a line of young trees on your left. Go through a wide wooden gate, and keep going across a field to a smaller gate ahead. Once through this head for the far right corner of the field, near houses, and go over a wooden stile next to a metal gate.

9. Go left and through another gate into a farmyard. Stay on the track as it bends round to the right, then left, then right again. Pass the first small turning to your left. After a few paces, on passing out of the farm complex, take the next turning left, by a barn, into a field via a wooden gate. Keep the field boundary and a strip of woodland on your left as you follow the path. Go through a wooden gate. Follow the track round to the left and then go right, keeping a post and rail fence on the left. Go through another wooden gate into a field. Walk straight over it bearing to the right of some oak trees in the field towards a minor road.

10. Go over a stile, cross the road and take the stone stile ahead into the next field. Keep walking ahead, aiming left of trees ahead. On coming level with the second oak tree, go left through a wide metal gate and then turn sharp right. After a few yards go through a gap between a fence and a water trough, taking you into the next field. Keep the hedge and tree line on your right. Soon you glimpse **Westonbirt School (A)** over to the right. Go through a metal kissing gate into the next field, and keep going in the same direction, aiming for the golf course car park in the distance. Go through a metal gate between a hedge and a wall. Bear slightly right downhill to reach a stile onto the golf course. Aim for the right hand side of the car park and pass through it. Follow the track to join a tarmac road keeping the golf course on your left.

11. After passing through the golf course entrance, you have a choice. To take the *optional extension through the village and arboretum, see the asterisked section after step 14. Otherwise, turn right through a wooden gate next to a cattle grid onto a drive through the grounds of Westonbirt School. At a junction with the drive from the main road to the school buildings (right), go straight on. (If the **Westonbirt School Gardens (B)** are open, you may turn right onto this drive to visit them.) Go straight across the drive, bear slightly left, keeping a copse on your right, soon to pass through a metal kissing gate in the fence ahead. Continue in the same direction, through a large field, aiming to pass between two oak trees in the distance. Head for a metal gate next to a line of trees and go through it. Then bear left towards the three-bar metal stile and the main road (A433) beyond which lies the Jack Hares Bar of the Hare & Hounds Hotel (tel. 01666-880233), and its walled garden. Cross this busy road with care. With the hotel behind you, continue left along a pavement to reach a crossroads.

View towards Westonbirt School from the south

12. Cross the road to reach a small wooden gate opposite, amid trees, then another, to pick up a footpath through some paddocks. Keep post and rail fencing on your right. Once over the last stile go straight on to meet a hedge and turn right onto the **Monarch's Way (C)**, keeping the hedge on your left. Continue walking with the hedge and tree line on your left for about 300 yards.

13. Go over the next stile you meet on your left and bear right slightly uphill to cross a stone stile in a hedge. Aim then for the top right corner of the next field and exit via another stone stile. Go right to join a wide grassy track keeping post and rail fencing on your left and a hedge on the right. Go straight on through a gap in a stone wall and continue in the same direction, keeping a hedge on the right. When you reach the corner of this field, go over a stone stile with wooden struts. Go straight across the next field towards a wooden stile. Continue towards a wide wooden gate slightly to the left of a copse.

14. Pass through a wooden gate and then a metal one. Go straight on as signposted, keeping a boundary on your left. Aim for the metal gate in the fence ahead walking in the direction of a house. Go through the gate next to the cattle grid by the house. You are now at the south western end of Longfurlong Lane. Continue along the lane for about 300 yards. **Highgrove House (D)**, not visible, is away to your right. Take the first footpath indicated right into a field and turn left downhill to follow the line of the field edge, and going broadly parallel with the lane. Follow the footpath over a series of stiles into a section of woodland. On reaching a stone wall, go left over a stile and bear right across the field to re-join Longfurlong Lane. Turn left at the end of Longfurlong Lane, go over the brook and then turn right into West Street to return to the car park.

*Optional extension: Continue ahead through Westonbirt village and straight over the crossroads. Soon, cross over the main road (A433) with care to pick up the bridleway opposite. Stay on this right

Up and over - Fly negotiates a stile on the Monarch's Way

Horse by the Monarch's Way near Highgrove

through the valley floor of the arboretum, finally bearing right uphill just before the far boundary to reach a wide wooden gate at the top on your left. Go through this and turn right onto the path (part of the Monarch's Way). Keep the arboretum boundary wall on your right, and soon cross a minor road to continue on the path in the same direction. Soon you enter a field. Keep going for about 200 yards, keeping a hedge on your left. Continue as instructed from step 13.

Notes:

A: **Westonbirt House** was the home of the Holford family for nearly three centuries. The Italian Renaissance style mansion seen today was built in 1863 by Robert Stayner Holford (1808-92) who began the arboretum with a collection of specimen trees planted in the grounds. His son, Sir George Holford, worked with him for more than 20 years to extend the tree collection into Silk Wood, an ancient semi-natural woodland. The 600-acre arboretum, of more than 18,000 specimen trees and shrubs from all over the world, is managed by the Forestry Commission (forestry.gov.uk/westonbirt), and supported by the Friends of Westonbirt Arboretum. After Sir George Holford's death, the house became a girls' school in 1928.

B: **Westonbirt School Gardens**: To create the formal gardens, Robert Holford had the entire village demolished and rebuilt a ¼ mile away. The Grade I Listed gardens are open to the public on certain summer days. To check opening times, telephone 01666-880333.

C: **The Monarch's Way** traces the flight of Charles II after the Battle of Worcester in 1651. Pursued by Oliver Cromwell's army, he travelled north then south through the Cotswolds, the Mendips to the south coast and along the South Downs to Shoreham before escaping to France. The 610-mile long trail links existing footpaths and bridleways.

D: **Highgrove House** was built in 1796-8, and re-built after a fire in 1893. The Prince of Wales bought the house and estate in 1980 from Maurice Macmillan, son of the former Conservative Prime Minister Harold Macmillan. Having embarked on a substantial renovation of the house, the Prince began converting the farm and gardens at Highgrove to organic methods in 1986.

12. LACOCK

Distance:	6 miles
Time:	3 hours
Pubs:	Red Lion, Lacock; Lysley Arms, Pewsham
Map:	OS Explorer 156: Chippenham & Bradford-on-Avon
Star-rating:	** Moderate
Start/End:	National Trust car park, Lacock ST 917682

This delightful route from Lacock through the countryside north east of the village takes you alongside the former Wilts and Berks canal up to Pewsham Locks and back over Naish Hill. A popular location for film and TV dramas, Lacock featured in Pride and Prejudice, and the Abbey Cloisters in the Harry Potter films. The Lysley Arms, about half way round, serves good food at reasonable prices and has plenty of space inside and out. Lacock lies about 12 miles south of Malmesbury (about 30 minutes drive), off the A350 Chippenham-Melksham road.

Route:

From the car park entrance cross the road and follow the gravel path. Turn left off the path onto a road into Lacock, passing the entrance to **Lacock Abbey (A)** and the **Fox Talbot Museum (B)** on your right. Take the first road on the right, East Street, opposite the Red Lion Inn (tel. 01249-730456), and at the end, turn right again towards the church. Once level with the church entrance go left down a no through road. Cross the packhorse bridge, bear right along the path past the stream and continue uphill to the top of the lane.

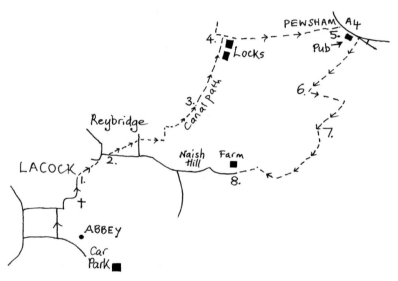

1.   Turn right through a wooden kissing gate and walk across a sloping field on the surfaced path. Once through another kissing gate, continue past houses at the hamlet of Reybridge to a road. Turn right and then right again along the stone bridge over the **River Avon (C)**.

2. After about 20 yards, take the stile left and walk diagonally right across the field. Exit the field via a metal stile next to a stone wall. Pick up the footpath on the other side of the road, and continue walking between two fences. Go over another pair of metal stiles into a field. Turn left following the left hand field edge as it bears round to the right. About half way along this long field edge, take the wooden stile to your left into another field. Turn right and keep going with a hedge line on your right to a stile at the highest point in the field onto a path through a thicket.

3. Exit the thicket via a stile and continue straight ahead to join a foot and cycle path, passing the route of the former **Wilts and Berks Canal (D)** on your right. After a few hundred yards you pass a bend in the River Avon on your left, and a restored canal bridge near a bench. Keep going for about ½ mile towards Pewsham Locks.

4. Look out for a footbridge spanning the last disused lock on your right. Cross this and a stile into a field. Keep to the left hand field edge. On the horizon ahead are Derry Hill and the western edge of **Bowood Park (E)**. Continue through a gap into another field. The right of way goes straight across the field to meet a farm track. If the path has disappeared under cultivation, turn left and keep going via the left hand field edge all the way round to meet the farm track. Bear left onto the track and

keep going to reach a T-junction with a main road (A4).

Footbridge, Pewsham Locks, south of Chippenham

5.   Turn right onto the pavement. The Lysley Arms (tel. 01249-652864) soon appears on your right after a garage. Keep going along the pavement and soon enter a cul-de-sac. After walking about 100 yards along this cul-de-sac, turn right by a telegraph pole onto a narrow surfaced lane, also a bridleway, which soon starts winding its way uphill.

6.   Just before reaching a big house on the hill, and just before coming level with some garages on your left, turn left to pass through a wide metal gate into a large field. Bear left keeping a wood on the left and a large field rising uphill away to your right, and

walk to the corner of the field. Turn right uphill keeping a field edge on your left.

7. Once in the next field, follow the path as it curves left along the field edge and then straightens out as it takes you uphill again. Continue in the same direction.

8. Near the top of the hill, join a farm road via a gate next to a cattle grid and continue to a T-junction. Turn right downhill and stay on the lane all the way back to the bridge over the Avon which you crossed at the end of step 1. Retrace your steps back into Lacock the way you came. You will see the Red Lion opposite the junction of East Street with the High Street. There's a National Trust café next to the pub.

Notes:

A: **Lacock Abbey**: Built for an order of Augustinian nuns, the Abbey became a family home after the Dissolution, and was donated to the National Trust by descendants of the Fox Talbot family in 1944. The Cloisters have featured in several Harry Potter films.

B: **Fox Talbot Museum**: Housed in a 16th century barn, the museum celebrates the life and work of Lacock's most famous resident William Henry Fox Talbot, who came to live at the Abbey in 1827. He invented the negative-positive photographic process, and used architectural features of the Abbey in many of his first photographic experiments.

South end of East Street, Lacock

C: **The River Avon:** Avon is an old English word meaning river. This is part of the Bristol Avon, which rises above Malmesbury (the Tetbury and Sherston branches meet east of Baskerville, Malmesbury) and meanders through Wiltshire and Somerset, via Chippenham, Melksham and Bath to the sea at Avonmouth, west of Bristol.

D: Built between 1795-1810 to connect the Thames at Abingdon with the Kennet & Avon Canal at Semington, the **Wilts and Berks Canal** (wbct.org.uk) is undergoing restoration for public access after falling into disuse nearly a century ago.

E: **Bowood Park:** About 100 acres of parkland surrounds Bowood House (bowood.org) the family seat of the Marquis and Marchioness of Lansdowne. Open to the public from April to October, the Bowood estate includes landscaped gardens designed by Capability Brown, a rhododendron walk and a much-praised children's adventure playground.

13. LITTLE SOMERFORD

Distance:	6 miles
Time:	3 hours
Pubs:	Rose & Crown, Lea; The Saladin, Little Somerford
Map:	OS Explorer 168: Stroud, Tetbury & Malmesbury
Star-rating:	** Moderate
Start/End:	Market Cross, Malmesbury ST 934873

Rich in railway interest, this walk from Malmesbury to Kingsmead Mill on the western edge of Little Somerford takes you via Lea and back past Cole Park. Mainly level, the route offers an optional extension into the centre of Little Somerford which adds 2 miles.

Route:

From the Market Cross, Malmesbury, and facing the High Street, turn left along Oxford Street. At a T-junction in front of Tower House, cross the road and turn right soon to pass the short stay car park (right) and the library (left). A few yards further on, turn left down Silver Street, past Ingram Street and down Back Hill steps.

1. Turn left, go over a river bridge and pass the bowls club on your left. As the road bends right - and just beyond a house called Watersmeet – the Sherston and Tetbury branches of the Avon join up. At the

end of the road, pass to the right of a wide metal barrier and continue in the same direction underneath the A429 Malmesbury by-pass on a metalled lane. Go over a cattle grid (or through the gate next to it) into a field. Continue ahead on the lane. Watch out for occasional vehicles. Where the lane bends left, note some remains of a railway bridge (left) once part of the Malmesbury branch line. Carry on to a Wessex Water site entrance.

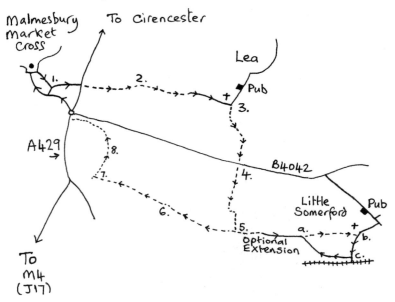

2. Turn right just before the entrance and go over the stile on the right to join a narrow tree-lined path running past the side of the sewage works. Go through a metal gate at the end of this path into a

field. Keep going in the same direction, gently uphill, keeping a hedge on your right. After the ground levels out you soon reach a stile on the right next to the end of the hedge. Cross the stile and walk downhill aiming for a bend in the farm lane visible near the bottom left corner of the field. Go through a wooden gate by the river to join the farm lane. Turn right and follow it as it bends left soon to pass between buildings. Stay on the lane through a field and then past some houses on the outskirts of Lea. On reaching a T-junction, turn left onto a pavement, cross over the entrance to Pembroke Green and pass St Giles Church. When you come level with the back of the church, you have a choice. If visiting the Rose & Crown pub (tel. 01666-824344) follow the pavement round to the left past

Pigeon in the tower – St Giles Church, Lea

the back of the church, and you will see the pub and garden on your left. If not visiting the pub, turn right, and cross the road to join a footpath via two white posts set at angle, near a yellow grit store.

3.　Continue along this narrow path soon to enter a field via a stile. Turn left and keep a boundary on the left for about 60 yards. Take the stile on your left, then turn right onto a path running between a double row of young trees (left) and a hedge (right). After crossing the next stile, walk diagonally left across a field along a clear path and go over the next stile into another field. Walk uphill – keeping a hedge on the left – and soon pass an electricity pole (left). Go through a metal gate next to a tree at the corner of the field and turn left. Ignore another metal gate on the left and walk a few paces towards a section of post and rail fence (three horizontal wooden rails and a large oak post). Climb over this, turn right and carry on keeping a barbed wire fence on the right. Head towards farm buildings along a grass strip and go left at the corner. Go through the first metal gate you see on your right, then another to join a track through a farmyard soon to reach a T-junction with the B4042 (Malmesbury-Swindon road).

4.　Cross the road and continue along the track opposite leading to **Maunditts Park Farm (A)**. On a clear day, there are fine views on the right towards the

Severn Vale and the Rodbourne water tower.
Continue straight ahead following the track into a
large sloping field, and through a gate into a second
field where the ground becomes level. Continue to a
gap in the trees ahead to reach a T-junction with
part of the route of the dismantled Malmesbury
branch railway. Turn left here to pass between trees
and hedges on either side and continue for about 60
yards to a wooden footbridge on your right. Turn
right across the footbridge and continue straight
ahead, keeping trees on your right at first, then post
and rail fencing. As the path bends left, you pass a
small copse on your left and see a bridge away to
your right. Soon you reach a junction of paths, with

*View across the Avon from the footpath
west of Kingsmead Mill*

a metal fence ahead of you and the river Avon just beyond it. Here you have a choice: to do the **optional extension*** into the centre of Little Somerford, adding 2 miles to your walk, see the directions after step 8. If not doing the extension, turn right here either through the gate or over the stile on your right.

5. Go straight across the field, and over the river bridge ahead of you through gates at each end. Follow a clear path soon to pass a large bend in the river on your right. You soon enter a clearing, passing between two lines of young trees, to emerge by a metal gate. Go through this into a large field and continue ahead, slightly left, towards a wide gap in the trees in the distance. Walk through the gap (it can be boggy at this spot next to the river), straight across the next field and aim for the far left corner. Go through a wooden gate in the corner and then over a stone footbridge across a junction of streams. Bear left, keeping a bend in the stream on your left. Where the stream straightens out, turn right across a field towards a wooden gate in the tree and hedge line.

6. Go through the gate and walk straight ahead up a gentle incline, keeping a hedge on your right and the cultivated area of a large field on your left. Go through a gap in the tree line ahead into the next field where the gradient becomes slightly steeper. Continue in the same direction through another gate,

over the brow of a hill and then straight on downhill past the ha-ha separating the gardens of **Cole Park (B),** away to your right, and the field. If there is electric fencing across the path near the ha-ha, you can step over the sheathed sections. Go over a stile into the next field, and continue straight on across a drive and over another stile in the fence ahead of you. Go diagonally left, and through a stand of trees. Continue in the same direction to exit the field via a stile set in a boundary fence in front of a tall evergreen hedge. Turn right onto a track and follow this as it bends left to reach a crossroads of tracks near farm buildings. Turn right here, pass a pond on your left and go through a gate.

7. Keep going on the track uphill with a hedge on the left, then once through a gateway, down the other side of the hill. Towards the bottom of the hill, just past a large oak tree near the hedge on your left, go across a stile in the hedge-line on your left. Continue along the bottom edge of the field. After passing the first large tree on your left, go over the stile on your right, and then a second one, to emerge into a sloping field.

8. Go straight along the top edge of the field, keeping a hedge on your left, towards the roofline of a large house. Go over a stile near the corner of the field and bear diagonally left uphill, passing a small fenced area of young trees on your left, to reach a stile at the brow of the hill. Cross the stile into the

next field. Follow the path gently downhill aiming well to the right of the new health centre and care home complex ahead. Pass through a wide wooden gate set in the fence ahead of you into the next field. Go diagonally right across the field and go over a stile in the corner. Go straight on, keeping a boundary on your right, over one last stile to join a track that takes you down to the main road (A429). Cross the road and bear right along the pavement. Go straight on across the entrance to Barley Close, and continue downhill passing houses on both sides, then the back of a bus shelter on the right. Just before reaching the road bridge, turn left onto a footbridge over the river, then turn right through a pair of wrought-iron gates. Turn left onto the pavement and walk along the High Street which soon bends right and takes you back up to the Market Cross.

* Optional extension

Turn left at the junction of paths, and keep going with the metal fence, and beyond it the river, on your right. Soon a high stone wall appears on your right, replacing the fence. After passing across a driveway keep going with a grass bank on your right and a track on the left. Go through a metal gate to emerge at the end of a lane. Beyond the gates on your right lies **Kingsmead Mill (C)**. The Little Somerford railway viaduct stretches across the horizon ahead of you beyond some young trees.

Turn left onto the lane and go past the former (railway) crossing-keeper's cottage on the left and over the site of **Kingsmead Crossing (D)**. Continue uphill under a tree canopy to reach a junction with a drive to a house on the left and a stile ahead of you into a field.

Railway viaduct from the western end of Mill Lane

a) Go over the stile and straight across the field towards a stile into a second field. Bear diagonally right across the second field to cross a third stile next to a gate. Go straight across the next field aiming for a high fence ahead, soon to pass a pond on your left. Keep the church tower in your sights as you aim for the far left corner of the field. Take the wooden stile to the left of a house and then a final stile ahead onto a narrow path. Continue ahead all the way to a road.

b) Turn left to reach the centre of Little Somerford. St John the Baptist Church soon appears on your left. The church contains a memorial to a famous balloonist Walter Powell, who was elected MP for Malmesbury in 1868. Powell was lost over the English Channel in the balloon Saladin in December 1881, never to be seen again. To reach the Saladin pub (tel. 01666-824222), continue past the church to reach a T-junction about 400 yards further on. Turn left at the junction and you will soon see the pub on your left. Retrace your steps past the church and the footpath you walked on earlier.

Village sign, Little Somerford

c) Just before reaching the railway bridge over the road, turn right into Mill Lane, passing the village hall on your right. Stay on Mill Lane past the former crossing-keeper's cottage, and retrace your steps past Kingsmead Mill all the way back to the spot where the optional extension begins. Go straight on over the stile or through the gate, and continue as described from point 5 above.

Notes:

A: **Maunditts Park** is thought to be of Norman origin and named after John Mauduit, Sheriff of Wiltshire and Governor of the Castle of Old Sarum in the reign of Edward III. It was a deer park for about three centuries from this time until Charles I's reign.

B: Originally owned by Malmesbury Abbey and known as Cowfold, **Cole Park** is a moated medieval manor house, parts of which date back to the latter half of the 16th century. After the Dissolution, the estate was granted to Edward Seymour, Duke of Somerset in 1548 and for much of the Tudor period it was a royal stud farm. The family of Hugh Audley, Sheriff of Wiltshire in 1654, owned it during the 17th century.

C: **Kingsmead Mill** operated as a working mill for many years under the ownership of the Fry family until 1961. Subsequent owners have included the film maker (Lord) David Puttnam, and the electrical appliances entrepreneur Sir James Dyson, whose company is Malmesbury's biggest employer.

D: **Kingsmead Crossing** was the mid-point of the Malmesbury branch railway line from Dauntsey

Lock. Bill Archard became crossing keeper in 1922 and he lived at the cottage until 1979. The crossing keeper's cottage remains. See the notes accompanying Walk 1 Lea for more information about the Malmesbury branch railway.

14. AVEBURY

Distance:	4 miles
Time:	2 hours
Refreshments:	Red Lion, Avebury & National Trust cafe
Map:	OS Explorer 157: Marlborough
Star-rating:	* Easy
Start/End:	National Trust car park, Avebury SU 099697

A relaxing walk through quintessential Wiltshire landscape and a stroll around the ancient stone circle, at the heart of the World Heritage Site. From Windmill Hill there are captivating views in all directions, notably of the Ridgeway, Silbury Hill, Cherhill Down and the Earl of Lansdowne monument. Starts and finishes at the visitors' car park (pay and display, free to National Trust members) in Avebury - about 10 miles south of Swindon off the A4361 Marlborough Road.

Route:

From the visitors' car park in Avebury, head towards the village along the waymarked footpath. Turn left when you reach the road, then right just past the church entrance, and at the end of that, left again onto a narrow lane. After passing a pumping station on the left, look out for Silbury Hill on your left, and go over a footbridge.

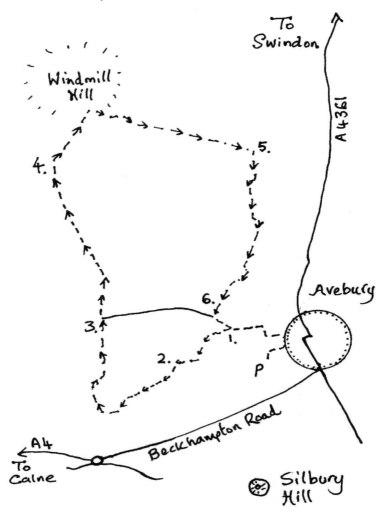

1. Where the footpath forks, take the left fork onto a section of the **Wessex Ridgeway (A)**. Go through the gate into a field and follow the metal fence on your left to exit the field near a house. Continue to a junction of tracks at **Avebury Trusloe (B)**.

2. Go straight on, and on reaching another road, continue straight ahead along a footpath through a pair of metal bars. At the end of this turn right onto a narrow road, and continue ahead past some cottages. **Longstones Field (C)**, excavated by a team of Southampton University archaeologists in 1999, soon appears on the right. Continue past two standing stones – the Adam and Eve stones – and follow the track round to the right, skirting the edge of the same field.

Adam and Eve stones, Longstones Field, Avebury Trusloe

3. After passing between two barns, go straight on at the junction of tracks to start ascending **Windmill Hill (D)**. As you approach the summit you get a better view of the Ridgeway over to your right, and of Cherhill Down and the Earl of Lansdowne monument, to the left. Soon you reach a gate on the right and a National Trust sign.

4. Pass through the gate onto Windmill Hill, and walk towards the right of the summit. Continue in the same direction to a gate and another National Trust sign on the other side of the field. Go through the gate and walk downhill keeping a metal fence, and later a hedgerow, on your left. Pass through a metal gate.

5. Just after the grass gives onto a metalled track, take the footpath signposted right into a field back towards Avebury. Cross to the next field via three stiles close together in a hedgerow. Continue in the same direction until you reach a footbridge. Cross this and turn left towards a stile ahead of you.

6. Turn left along the path and retrace your steps back into Avebury. To visit the Red Lion (tel. 01672-539266) continue past the path leading back to the car park. The pub is at the top of the road on the left. Access to the stone circle is via several gates around the village.

Lychgate & church tower, Avebury

*Part of the Avebury stone circle and
World Heritage Site*

Notes:

A: **Wessex Ridgeway** is a 136-mile route from Marlborough to Lyme Regis devised by the Ramblers' in the mid 1980s. It joins the Ridgeway National Trail – an 85-mile route from nearby Overton Hill to Ivinghoe Beacon, Buckinghamshire – about 2 miles north east of Avebury.

B: **Avebury Trusloe:** After the heir to a Scottish marmalade fortune Alexander Keiller bought much of the village in the 1930s, and embarked on his famous excavations of the circle, many of the older cottages within it were demolished. It was decided that new buildings should be restricted to Avebury Trusloe in order to protect the integrity of the stone circle.

C: **Longstones Field:** William Stukeley, an 18th century historian, proposed the existence of a prehistoric "Beckhampton Avenue" of paired megaliths into the Avebury stone circle, similar to the West Kennett avenue still evident today to the east of the village. An excavation here by the Southampton University team in 1999 provided the best evidence to date that Stukeley was right. They found evidence of three buried stones, and three pits where stones had either been removed or burned. (Walk 15: Silbury Hill takes you through West Kennett Avenue.)

D: **Windmill Hill** has the earliest-known enclosed Neolithic settlement in the area, revealed in excavations in the 1920s led by Alexander Keiller and thought to date back 5,500 years. Evidence suggests these early settlers not only kept cattle, sheep, pigs, goats and dogs and grew crops but also made pottery – hence the name given to them, the Beaker People.

15. SILBURY HILL

Distance:	5 miles
Time:	2.5 hours
Refreshments:	Red Lion pub, National Trust café, Avebury
Map:	OS Explorer 157: Marlborough
Star-rating:	** Moderate
Start/End:	National Trust car park Avebury SU 099697

Rich in prehistoric sites, exquisite downland views, and landscape interest, this is a rewarding walk all year round. You may see a crop circle in the summer. The hay and straw bales in the fields at harvest time complement the ancient standing stones. Mainly level with one or two moderate inclines. Park at the National Trust visitors' car park off the A4361 at Avebury.

Route:

Turn right out of the car park entrance away from the village. After 40 yards cross the main road opposite a signposted bridleway. Pass through a wooden gate and continue on this path with a fence on your left and a stream running along a ditch on the right. Pass through a pair of gates, from which **Silbury Hill (A)** is visible on the right; then cross over a pair of stiles. Continue in the same direction to meet the main road (A4).

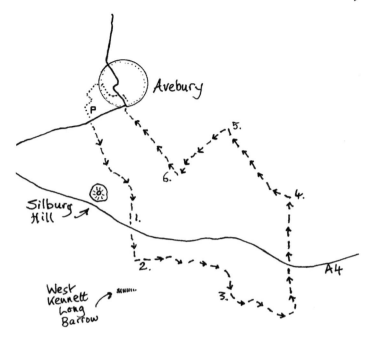

1. Cross the road with care, turn left and almost immediately right onto a path. After going over a footbridge, go left through a kissing gate keeping a field and a hill on your right. To visit the **West Kennett Long Barrow (B)**, turn right at the corner of the field and walk straight up the hill. If not visiting the long barrow keep going ahead on the path along the valley.

2. Go straight on over a minor road, keeping a field boundary on your right. Soon you cross a stile into a small woodland.

113

3. At a T-junction of paths turn left onto a bridleway. On reaching a road, turn left, go over a bridge, and then almost immediately right. Keep to the field edge on your right. When you reach another T-junction of paths, you should see the tower of West Overton church ahead. Turn left uphill. Before crossing the main road (A4), look out for the site of a prehistoric shrine called the **Sanctuary (C)** on your left, and a good view of Silbury Hill. Once over the road continue on the **Ridgeway (D)** up Overton Hill, past three burial mounds on your right, for about ½ mile.

Silbury Hill from the A4 near West Kennett Long Barrow

4. Take the first path left, signposted a byway. Once past a stand of beech trees, you should be able to see the tower of Avebury church ahead and the West Kennett stone avenue away to your left.

5.   Continue downhill on the path for about ¼ of a mile. Then the path starts rising gently uphill. After about 150 yards of gentle uphill walking, take the footpath left along a field edge, keeping a fence on your right, soon to reach a road. Cross the road and pass through the wooden gate on the right.

Walkers on the bank above the stone circle, Avebury

6.   Turn right and pass through **West Kennett Avenue (E)**. At the end of the Avenue, cross the road again, to pass through a gate leading to the Avebury stone circle. Follow the henge round to your left to reach the Red Lion (tel. 01672-539266). Alternatively bear left and follow the line of the road, to cross it once more half way down the field. This takes you

into towards the centre of the village, the National Trust restaurant and shop, public toilets, Avebury Manor and the Museum.

Notes:

A: **Silbury Hill** is Europe's largest man-made pre-historic mound, standing around 40 yards high. Several early Wiltshire writers link its origins to the nearby rising of the River Kennet at Swallowhead Springs, a few hundred yards to the south. Others suggest that it was built as a monument to the Celtic goddess Sul, or as a giant sundial.

B: **West Kennett Long Barrow** is one of the best known Neolithic earthen mounds constructed for multiple burials. A bigger one is at East Kennett, unexcavated and lacking a public right of way to it.

C: **The Sanctuary**: Some 5,000 years ago a timber shrine was erected here later replaced by a double stone circle, linked by an avenue of stones to a new stone circle at Avebury.

D: **The Ridgeway** stretches from Overton Hill near Avebury to Ivinghoe Beacon in the Chilterns. It was used as a drovers' road or trading route at least since the bronze age. An 85-mile long national trail, incorporating most of the ancient road, was created in the early 1970s.

E: **West Kennett Avenue** is widely supposed to have been built as a processional route for Neolithic people visiting Avebury for ritual gatherings; the alternating shapes of the standing stones, upright columnar stones then wide, flat ones, are thought to represent male and female figures.

16. ASHTON KEYNES

Distance:	6 miles
Time:	3 hours
Pubs:	Baker's Arms, Somerford Keynes
	White Hart Inn, Ashton Keynes
Map:	OS Explorer 169: Cirencester &
	Swindon
Star-rating:	** Moderate
Start/End:	Neigh Bridge car park, Somerford
	Keynes SU 018946

Riverbanks, lakes and abundant wildlife are the themes of this tranquil and level walk through part of the Cotswold Water Park from Somerford Keynes to Ashton Keynes via the Thames Path. Plenty of bird-spotting opportunities. The walk starts and finishes at Neigh Bridge car park, Somerford Keynes, a 15-minute drive (8 miles) from Malmesbury, via Crudwell and Oaksey.

Route:

From Neigh Bridge Country Park car park pass a bike park and children's play area and head for the lakeside. Turn right and keep the lake on your left soon enter woodland and join the Thames Path. Once on the path, you see the lake through trees on your left and the river on your right.

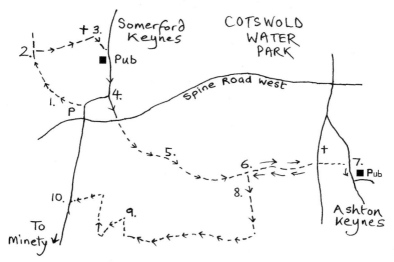

1. At the far end of the lake turn right off the lakeside path over a wooden footbridge into a field. Follow the left hand field edge keeping the hedge and river on your left. The path soon bends to the left. At the end of the field go through a gate. Ignore a footbridge going over the river to Kemble Mill, and instead keep going straight on until you reach a clear grassed path on your right going straight across the middle of the field.

2. Take this right turn across the field. At the far end of the field cross a footbridge to enter parkland. Go straight ahead and, in the middle of the field, bear slightly left to follow the path to a gate.

3. On reaching the corner of the field just to the right of the church, pass through a wooden gate and follow the footpath ahead. Continue along the footpath keeping a high stone wall on your right, and a row of trees on your left. Turn left onto a gravel drive past cottages to reach a road. Cross over the road and turn right onto a pavement to walk through Somerford Keynes village. The Baker's Arms (tel. 01285-861298) is on the right.

Lakeside homes, Lower Mill Estate - viewed from the Thames Path

4. As the road bends right, turn left into Mill Lane and at the end cross the main road to pick up the lane opposite. After a few yards, turn left onto a lakeside path. The lakes you see on this walk form part of the **Cotswold Water Park (A)**. Soon, on your right you

pass some of the homes built on the **Lower Mill Estate (B)**. At the end of the path, join the metalled road for about 50 yards and then continue ahead on the track.

5. On approaching a wooden gate ahead, cross the metal footbridge on your right over the Thames and follow the path as it bends left.

6. At a junction of footpaths, continue straight ahead towards Ashton Keynes. (To shorten the walk by a couple of miles, you can turn right here onto a path and follow the route directions from step 8 below.) Cross over a road and continue towards **Ashton Keynes (C)**, keeping the river on your left.

7. On reaching a T-junction, turn right to reach the White Hart Inn (tel. 01285-861247), which has a pleasant garden. Retrace your steps back along the Thames Path to the junction of footpaths mentioned at step 6. Turn left to follow the signposted path.

8. Stay on the track between Freeth Mere on your right and a hedge on your left. You are walking along the eastern edge of the Lower Mill estate nature reserve. Follow the track, which soon bends right towards a wooden footbridge. After crossing the footbridge, follow the footpath as it bears right across a meadow keeping a fence, and just beyond it Swill Brook, on your left.

Belted Galloway cattle, Lower Mill Estate

9. On reaching another footbridge follow the waymarked path through woods and the **Swillbrook Lakes Nature Reserve (D)**.

10. On reaching a road, go through the kissing gate and turn right along a quiet road. At the junction with the spine road, cross over the road to return to the Neigh Bridge Country Park car park.

Notes:

A: The **Cotswold Water Park** (waterpark.org) is the largest of its kind in the UK – bigger than the Norfolk Broads – and still growing. More than 130 lakes have been created, out of former gravel pits, across 40 square miles. A haven for wildlife, it offers a wealth of leisure and educational opportunities – water sports, cycling and walking, angling, bird-watching and conservation activities.

B: Described by one commentator as a "brave new ghetto for weekenders...an exercise in social engineering", **Lower Mill Estate** claims to be the UK's first "residential nature reserve". Former publishing tycoon Jeremy Paxton's innovative development combines entrepreneurial flair with a passion for conservation and wildlife.

The Thames at Ashton Keynes

C: **Ashton Keynes** is an attractive little village with dainty footbridges spanning the shallow Thames. Refugees from Nazi Germany and elsewhere in mainland Europe fled here in the 1930s to form the Cotswold Bruderhof, also known as the Hutterian Brethren. A closed community of pacifist

Christians, they farmed 300 acres for many years and lived a simple, frugal life. Ever resourceful, they built a power station and hospital and carried out printing and bookbinding. In the 1940s, the Community relocated to Primavera, a rural backwater of Paraguay.

D: **Swillbrook Lakes Nature Reserve** provides flourishing habitats to a host of summer migrant and over-wintering birds, dragonflies and damson flies, and wildflowers. The reserve is run by the Wiltshire Wildlife Trust. (wiltshirewildlife.org).

17. AVENING

Distance:	6 miles
Time:	3 hours
Pubs:	Weighbridge Inn, Minchinhampton
	Bell Inn, Avening
Map:	OS Explorer 168: Stroud, Tetbury &
	Malmesbury
Star-rating:	** Moderate
Start/End:	Avening High Street, near Post Office
	and Stores

Gently undulating landscape and woodland – plus the benefit of an excellent pub just over half way along the route – make this a good walk for all seasons. Views of Gatcombe Park, home of the Princess Royal, add interest on the return leg. Starts and finishes in the attractive Cotswold village of Avening, whose church owes its origins to Matilda, William the Conqueror's queen. Parking is available in Avening High Street. The village lies 3 miles north of Tetbury on the B4014, and is within about 15 minutes drive from Malmesbury.

Route:

From the Post Office and Stores in Avening High Street, walk downhill and take the first turning left Point Road just before a phone box. Ignore the turning to Pound Hill and continue to a T-junction. Turn left and follow the road as it narrows to a single-track lane, soon passing a no through road sign. There are pleasant views across the valley here.

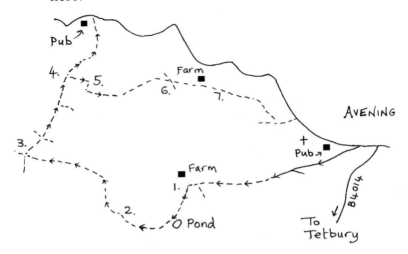

1. At the bottom of the hill, go past the bridleway waymarked to the left, but take the "restricted byway" to the left a few paces further on along a metalled drive. About 50 yards after leaving the road, take the footpath diversion to your left through a wooden gate. Turn right onto a grassy path. Go over a wooden footbridge ahead, and then a stile with a dog door to the side. Turn left, keeping a stream on your left. Follow the footpath along the bottom of the valley, with a hedge and trees on your left. Keep going past a pond (left) as the path bends right.

2. Continue straight towards trees ahead and pass through a gate. The path rises gently uphill with a plantation on your right. Follow the footpath signs across fields, keeping a boundary on your left, before reaching a junction of paths in a wooded area.

Farm and hillsides, east of Avening

3. Turn right onto a track (marked on the OS map as Shipton Graves Lane) and continue along this, mostly through woods. You may be able to see the Wiltshire Downs on the distant horizon (right). Half a mile further on, at a second junction of paths, bear left through the second metal gate on the left (with a blue arrow marker on the gatepost). On reaching another patch of woodland, Hazel Wood, you reach a third junction of paths.

4. Here you can choose to: **a)** visit the Weighbridge Inn (tel. 01453-832520), about 10 minutes walk from here. Go straight on downhill, following a track that borders a small stream. Go straight across a field, keeping to the right of the stream, and then back into woodland, towards a road. If the track is muddy, there are alternative paths either side. Go through a metal gate onto a road. Cross the road with care, and turn left onto a pavement. The pub is about 20 yards down the road to your left. Retrace your steps back to the crossroads of paths and go left just before the gate. **b)** skip the pub visit – simply turn right at this junction of paths. Now you have Hazel Wood on your left and a field on the right.

Pub sign

5.   Follow the path alongside the top edge of Hazel Wood. Cut right soon, via a wooden kissing gate, then follow the path round to the left to pass fields on the right. After about ¼ mile, fork left, as indicated, back into woodland to re-join the track you walked on earlier.

6.   At the next junction of tracks, go straight ahead downhill through a wide metal gate. Continue on the track downhill with a few trees on the left and a grassy bank rising to the right. Keep going on the track between oak trees. On reaching farm buildings, go through a metal gate and continue straight ahead through another gate into a field.

7.   Continue in the same direction across the field to pass through a third gate onto a narrow path. Keep a stone wall on your left and a hedge on the right. There are fine views on your left towards **Gatcombe Park (A)**, home of HRH the Princess Royal. Soon you join a wider track coming from your right. Continue walking downhill back into the village. Turn right back into Avening High Street. Just before the Bell Inn (tel. 01453-836422), turn right to pass the school if you wish to visit **Holy Cross Church (B)** and **Churchyard (C)**.

Notes:

A: **Gatcombe Park:** The manor house was built between 1771-74. In 1979, the Queen bought the house and 730-acre estate for Princess Anne and

Captain Mark Phillips, who grew up in Great Somerford near Malmesbury. The royal couple hosted the first Gatcombe horse trials here in 1983 and the annual event continues to attract worldwide interest. The Princess Royal now lives in the manor with her second husband Rear-Admiral Timothy Laurence. Zara Phillips, daughter of the Princess and Capt Phillips, received an OBE in the 2007 New Year's Honours List after being named BBC Sports Personality of the Year.

Holy Cross Church, Avening

B: **Holy Cross Church, Avening** is considered one of the most important Norman churches in the Cotswolds, built by Queen Matilda, wife of William the Conqueror. Before meeting William, Matilda fell in love with a young lord called Brittic, who then held Avening Court. He spurned her advances. After her marriage to William and his accession to the English throne as William I, she took her revenge. Matilda persuaded the King to have Brittic imprisoned at Worcester, where he died. In remorse, she had Avening Church built so that prayers could be said for his soul. Its consecration on September 14th 1080, when the royal couple gave a boar's head to the villagers, continues to be celebrated on Pig Face Day.

C: **Holy Cross Churchyard:** Michael Powell (1905-1990), co-creator with Emeric Pressburger of such wartime British film classics as *A Matter of Life and Death, Black Narcissus* and *The Life and Death of Colonel Blimp* is buried near the eastern boundary of the graveyard. Engraved on a simple headstone is the epitaph: "Film director and optimist". His grave is next to that of the actress Pamela Brown, who appeared in many of Powell and Pressburger's films and lived with Powell in the village for many years. She died in 1975.

18. BOX HILL

Distance:	4 miles
Time:	2 hours
Pub:	The Quarryman's Arms, Box Hill
Map:	OS Explorer 156: Chippenham
Star-rating:	** Moderate
Starts/Finishes:	Selwyn Hall car park, Box ST 824 686

This charming and varied walk takes you east and north of Box, uphill through woodland across farmland and past Hazelbury Manor, parts of which date back to the 15th century. It's well worth the climb for the great views across the By Brook valley from Box Hill Common and the Quarryman's Arms. You return to Box along the side of the valley and the walk concludes with glimpses of Isambard Kingdom Brunel's famous Box Tunnel entrance.

Route:

From the car park walk up to the main road (A4) turn left onto a pavement and keep going towards the centre of Box. On reaching the post office and stores (left), cross the road and go up Bulls Lane. Continue uphill past the first road junction.

1. After the road gives onto a stony track, go straight on at a junction of paths to join a bridleway going downhill through woodland. At the next crossroads

of paths, continue ahead along a path that soon
bends right.

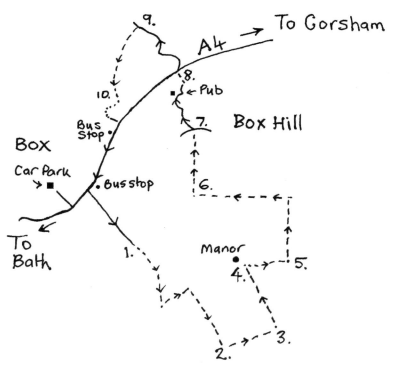

2.   Emerge from the woods into a field and follow a
wide grassed path (still a bridleway) as it turns left
uphill. Keep a field boundary on your left. There are
good views to your right and behind you. Soon you
meet a metalled drive leading to Hazelbury Manor.

View across the valley from Box Hill towards Colerne

GWR bench, Box Hill

3. Turn left and pass through a small wooden gate next to the large entrance gates and continue on one of the verges bordering the drive to the Manor.

4. At a junction of paths in front of the Manor entrance, turn right onto a metalled bridleway through mixed woodland. You may see parts of a topiary garden to your left. Continue past a metal barn on your left, soon going gently uphill.

5. Where the path starts going downhill again, turn left through a gap in the tree line onto a clear footpath going straight across the middle of a field. Exit the field via a gap in a stone wall. Turn left. Continue with a stone wall on your left along a grass path. On the centre left horizon you can see Kingsdown Hill.

6. Continue straight on towards woodland ahead and follow the path as it bends right along the edge of the wood, keeping a boundary and beyond it a field on your right. Just before you emerge from the woods you are walking over the route of the Box Tunnel.

7. On meeting a road junction, cross the road and continue in the same direction to the left of a grass triangle along a lane that passes benches on **Box Hill (A)** (right) and Grove Farm and the Quarryman's Arms (both left). Continue downhill from the pub along Barnetts Hill, cross over a minor road and the stone stile ahead soon to reach a main road (A4).

8. Cross the road with care and continue ahead over another stone stile into a steeply descending field. Keep the hedgerow on your left before exiting the field via a wooden stile. Continue downhill along a minor road.

Box Tunnel, Bath entrance

9. At the foot of the hill turn left and pass stone houses on each side. (If you cross over the river, you've gone too far.) Pass a parking area on your left and follow a grass path alongside a stream (right). Cross over the stream and a stile beyond it into a field. Continue straight on following a line of electricity

poles. Exit the field via a stile half way up the side of the hill. Follow the path uphill keeping a hedge on your left. Cross into the next field via a stile. Keep going past a post and rail fence on your left.

10. As the driveway bends left uphill, turn right and cross a stile into a paddock. Follow the path across the middle of the paddock and go over another stile onto another driveway. Continue ahead, slightly right, and follow the drive as it bends left. Go through a waymarked gate to join a road. Follow the road straight uphill between houses soon to reach a T-junction with the A4. Turn right onto a pavement. Pass a bus stop and shelter on your right (for eastbound services to Corsham and Chippenham). Cross the road to see the **Box Tunnel entrance (B)** from the viewing area or stay on the pavement to see the tunnel entrance on your left from the road bridge over the main line. Continue along the road past the post office to return to the car park at **Box (C)**.

Notes:

A. **Box Hill:** Limestone quarries were worked here from the 8th century to create the distinctive honey-coloured Bath stone characteristic of the area. By the 19th century, the underground workings spread almost as far as Corsham. Parts of this complex of quarries were requisitioned by the War Department during World Wars I and II for storage, and a huge subterranean military base continued to operate here through the Cold War. For many years it was Whitehall's main nuclear bunker. The Quarryman's Arms, mentioned in numerous good pub guides, is especially popular amongst cavers, walkers, and the odd UFO watcher. Its walls are covered with quarrying memorabilia.

B. **Box Tunnel:** It took five years (1836-41), some 1200 navvies and 400 horses to build this 3,312-yard long tunnel for Brunel's Great Western Railway. Each navvy got through a ton of gunpowder and candles per week to blast their way through the stone, often in foul weather. More than 100 navvies died in accidents during the tunnel's construction. The elegant classic design of the Bath portal, framed by the magnificent backdrop of fields and woodland rising behind, creates a memorable sight. Corsham-based Rudloe Stoneworks has produced a Box Tunnel cast stone fireplace surround - there's one at the Quarryman's Arms, another at Chippenham railway station cafe.

C: **Box** has several famous residents, past and present. The Rev. Wilbert V. Awdry (1911-1997), author of the *Thomas the Tank Engine* books, spent most of his childhood in the village. He is said to have been inspired to write the stories by the sounds of the railway engines "talking to each other" as they came in and out of Box station just a few hundred yards from his father's vicarage. Ex-Genesis star Peter

Gabriel created his Real World Studios in the village near the By Brook in the late 1980s, and the explorer David Hempleman-Adams also lives in Box.

19. EWEN

Distance:	5 miles
Time:	2½ hours
Pubs:	Wild Duck, Ewen; Baker's Arms, Somerford Keynes
Map:	OS Explorer 169: Cirencester & Swindon
Star-rating:	* Easy
Start/End:	Neigh Bridge Country Park car park SU 018 946

An easy-going level walk along the Thames Path from Neigh Bridge to the splendid 16th century inn at Ewen and then back along a pleasant grassy track and quiet country lanes via Somerford Keynes. Look out for spring and summer-flowering plants along this section of mainly shallow and crystal clear river. Start and finish at Neigh Bridge Country Park lakeside car park, near Somerford Keynes, a 15-minute drive (8 miles) from Malmesbury, via Crudwell and Oaksey.

Route:

From Neigh Bridge car park head towards the lakeside and turn right, keeping the water's edge on your left, soon to enter woodland and join the **Thames Path (A)**. Once on the path, you see the lake through trees on your left and the Thames on your right.

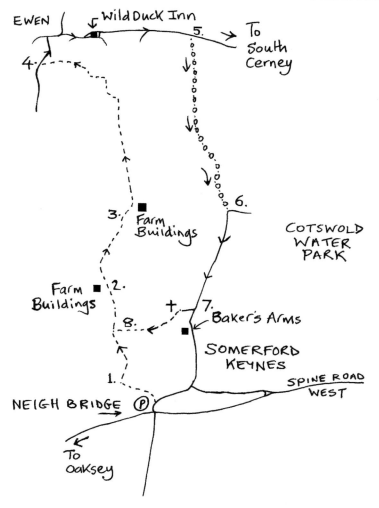

1.   At the far end of the lake turn right off the lakeside path over a wooden footbridge and through a metal kissing gate into a field. Follow the left hand field edge keeping the hedge and river on your left. At the end of the field go through a gate and continue in the same direction through a second and then a third field.

2. Go through another metal kissing gate and keep going past farm buildings on your left. About 300 yards after the buildings, follow the path as it bends right past a footbridge on your left. Exit this fourth field via another kissing gate and continue on the path towards more farm buildings (Upper Mill Farm).

3. Just before these buildings, turn left over the river via a footbridge (signposted Ewen 1 mile) and then follow the path as it bends right. Keep the river on your right (all the way to the start of step 4 below) and continue through the next kissing gate and over two stiles. Ignore a wooden gate you see at the corner of a field, just in front a bend in the river, or river bed, if dry. Instead follow the field boundary past some electricity pylons on your left, as the river meanders towards Ewen. Pass through a kissing gate to exit the field with the pylons in it and continue on the path, with trees on your left until you reach a road.

4. Turn right along the road, as it bends right and then left up an incline to meet a T-junction. Cross over

Swans on the Thames at Ewen

Green lane, heading for Somerford Keynes

the road, turn right onto a pavement and continue through Ewen, ignoring a left turning (signposted Siddington and Coates). Go past the front of the Wild Duck Inn (thewildduckinn.co.uk, tel. 01285-770310). To visit the inn, turn right at the next junction, signposted Somerford Keynes and Oaksey, and after a few yards right again through the car park entrance. If not visiting the inn continue along the road passing the front of the inn in the direction of South Cerney and Ashton Keynes. There are grass verges you can walk on if necessary. Pass a large house on your right and continue for about 300 yards.

5. Turn right onto a wide grassy track with a tree and hedge line on each side and keep going for about a mile.

6. On reaching a T-junction with a road, turn right towards Somerford Keynes. You can walk on the grass verges. Continue for about ½ mile to the northern edge of **Somerford Keynes (B)**.

7. After passing the speed restriction signs, take the first turning right along a lane signposted parish church – or continue ahead to visit the Baker's Arms (tel. 01285-861298) near the centre of the village. About 200 yards further along the lane, go left over a stone stile onto a footpath passing the eastern boundary of the churchyard (right) and a hedge (left). At a junction of paths, in front of a large house (Somerford House), turn right. Go through a kissing gate, next to an entrance to All Saints churchyard, to enter a large meadow. Follow the path diagonally left across the meadow and cross a footbridge into a large field. Continue straight across the field following a grass path running between two cultivated areas.

8. At the other side of the field, turn left to re-join the Thames Path. Return to the car park the way you came or go round the lake to reach it.

Notes:

A: The **Thames Path** extends 180 miles from its source at Trewsbury Mead between Kemble and Coates in the Cotswolds to the Thames barrier in east London. Little more than a stream for the first few miles, the river becomes navigable at Lechlade. The Thames Path was given national trail status in 1996.

B: Evidence of Iron Age and Roman settlement at **Somerford Keynes** was unearthed during excavations at Spratsgate Lane in the mid 1980s. The earliest written record of the village, in a charter dated 685 AD, mentioned a gift of 40 hides of land given by Bertwald, a nephew of King Ethelred, to Aldhelm, first abbot of Malmesbury. The Grade II Listed Church of All Saints is Saxon in origins was largely rebuilt in the 13th century. The tower was added in the early 18th century.

Snowdrops at Somerford Keynes

20. GATCOMBE PARK

Distance:	3 miles
Time:	1¾ hours
Pubs:	The Bell Inn, The Cross Inn, Avening
Map:	OS Explorer 168: Stroud, Tetbury & Malmesbury
Star-rating:	** Moderate
Start/End:	Avening High Street near Post Office ST 883979

This short walk across the high ground north of Avening offers sumptuous views towards Minchinhampton and Nailsworth. You go along the western edge of Gatcombe Park, home of the Princess Royal; and return to Avening via a hilltop golf course, and the boundary of another (one time) royal residence. There are two moderate inclines – one at the start and the other on the return leg. Avoid this walk during the Gatcombe Horse Trials (first week of August) when Steps Lane is temporarily closed. Avening lies about 3 miles north of Tetbury on the B4014, and is within about 15 minutes drive of Malmesbury. Park on the same side of the road as the Post Office and stores in Avening.

Route:

Cross the road and walk all the way down Avening High Street passing the Bell Inn (tel. 01453-836422)

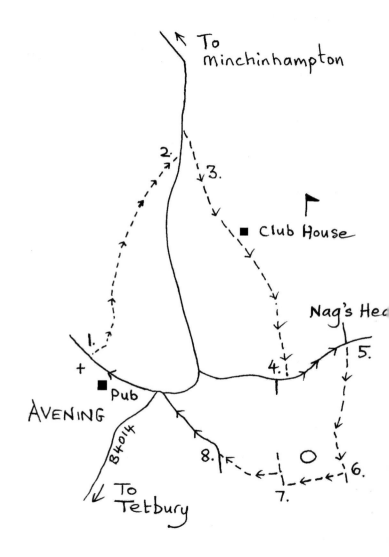

on your left and follow the road as it bends round to the right. (To visit **Holy Cross Church (A)** take a turning on your left past the memorial hall and school.) Opposite the red Avening village sign turn right up Rectory Lane.

1. Take the next turning to the left, opposite a pair of electricity poles, up a narrow metalled path (Steps Lane), keeping an old stone wall on your right. This takes you through woods and then part of **Gatcombe Park (B)** cross-country course. Continue along the lane to a road junction.

White Park cattle near Steps Lane, north of Avening

2. Turn left and after about 80 yards, cross the road with care and go over a stone stile in the wall into a

field. Go right, heading for another stone stile at the corner of a stone wall ahead. Go over this, and continue ahead keeping the field edge on your immediate right.

3.   On reaching the far right corner of the field, cross over a third stone stile onto a golf course. The right of way is clearly signposted – follow the yellow tipped waymarked posts across the course. Aim for the right hand side of the clubhouse straight ahead, but before reaching it go to the right of a hedge then keep going to pass between the covered practice area and the clubhouse. Continue between a hedge (left) and a car park (right), and at the far left corner go through a gap in the hedge towards a low stone wall ahead. Cross a drive and bear left of a hedge ahead of you. Go straight on with the hedge on your right. Ignore the first gap in the hedge on your right (near a large cylinder) but pass through the second gap right and then turn left onto a track leading to a grassed area. Go straight on for about 30 yards. After passing a clump of trees on your right bear diagonally right onto a grassed corridor soon going downhill towards a tree-lined valley.

Exit the golf course via a wooden stile into a sloping field and a plantation of young trees. Follow the path downhill towards a "walk through" metal stile onto a road. On the other side of the valley ahead you may see part of the landscaped grounds of **Avening Court (C)**.

4.   Once over the stile, turn left along the lane and through the hamlet of **Nag's Head** to reach a road junction before a red telephone box.

5.   Turn right onto a well-defined path, go through a metal gate and bear right uphill, keeping trees and a small brook on your right. Pass through another metal gate, and proceed along the path with trees on each side. After the path becomes level, continue past a field on the right with a large stand of trees in the middle of it – marked on the OS map as Roundabout.

Leaving the golf course on the way to Nag's Head

6.   Go right over a stone stile just beyond the end of this field, and continue walking, keeping a hedgerow and stone wall on your right and, beyond these, the stand of trees mentioned above. On

reaching the end of this field, go over another stone stile and emerge onto a track.

7. Turn right here and, after about 150 yards, turn left over a stone stile and follow the path straight across a field. After going over another stile, the path soon bears right across a field. Exit the field via a wooden stile in the far right corner.

8. Turn right onto a lane going downhill. At the bottom of the lane, next to the Cross Inn, cross the road and walk back down Avening High Street.

Notes:

A: **Holy Cross Church, Avening and B: Gatcombe Park**. See the notes accompanying Walk 17 Avening.

B: **Avening Court** is mentioned in the Domesday Book. William the Conqueror (William I) and Queen Matilda are said to have had Holy Cross Church built while they were living at Avening Court.

21. BARBURY CASTLE

Distance:	7½ miles
Time:	3½ hours
Pubs:	The Crown Inn & The Bell, Broad Hinton
Map:	OS Explorer 157: Marlborough
Star-rating:	*** More challenging
Start/End:	Hackpen Hill free car park, Ridgeway SU 129747

This bracing trek starts along part of the Ridgeway on the northern edge of the spectacular Wiltshire Downs, and then takes you around an Iron Age hill fort. You then descend to the hamlet of Uffcott and the village of Broad Hinton. The path back up to your starting point offers views of the Broad Hinton White Horse. There's little shade or shelter along this route, so perhaps it's best avoided during very hot weather or when heavy rain is forecast. The walk starts and ends at the Hackpen Hill free car park on the Ridgeway, about 2 miles south east of Broad Hinton.

Route:

From Hackpen Hill car park, head east along the Ridgeway in the direction of a big clump of beech trees, with far reaching views away to your left.

1. Once past the beech trees, ignore the bridleway signposted left to Broad Hinton and stay on the

track up a gentle incline, soon to pass a second clump of trees. As the track becomes level, old aircraft hangars on the site of the former RAF Wroughton airfield can be seen in the valley on your left. The **Science Museum (A)** now occupies part of this complex. Continue ahead to reach a junction of tracks right by the foot of Barbury Down.

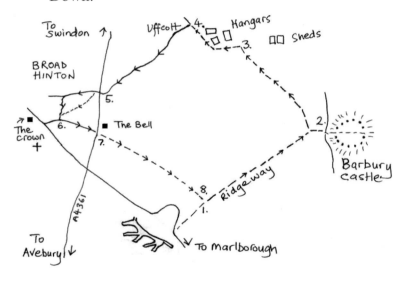

2. Turn right and then left through a gate onto Barbury Down. Proceed uphill along a clear path through the country park to **Barbury Castle (B)**. You can follow the path across the middle of the hill-fort, but for the best views north west towards the Cotswold Hills, and south across the downs towards

Marlborough, take the circular path left that takes you along the outer ramparts all the way round and back to your starting point. Retrace your steps down the path you came up back to the Ridgeway, turning right at the gate and then left – as if returning to Hackpen Hill car park. After about 300 yards, take the first right signposted byway onto a track in the direction of some hangars and metal sheds ahead. Continue downhill on the track.

View towards Hackpen Hill from the Ridgeway

3. After about a mile stay on the track as it bends left and then shortly right. At the gated entrance, on your right, to the site containing three large old aircraft hangars you reach a junction of paths. Go straight on.

Morning mist, Barbury Castle

4. On reaching a road junction, go left to pass through Uffcott. Note the interesting thatched chalk wall on your left, once used to accommodate bee-hives. Continue along this quiet road for about a mile, past a duck pond on your right, an equestrian centre and another pond on the left. On a clear day you should be able to see the Broad Hinton White Horse on your left.

5. At a crossroads, walk over the main road (A4361 Swindon to Marlborough) with care, and continue ahead a few paces to reach a stile on the left into a field. Here you have a choice: **a)** follow the right of way through the fields into Broad Hinton or **b)** take an alternative route following roads and alleyways.

a) The stile into the field on your left, and another later on, may be difficult to cross. However if you do get over it, bear sharp right across the field to meet a pair of stiles separated by a farm track. Once over these, bear diagonally left to the far top corner of the field. Go through a wide gate and after about 40 yards, turn right over a stile in the hedge onto a tarmac path. Turn left and follow the footpath round to meet some metal bars. After passing the first set of bars, turn left onto a track that brings you to a road. Turn right along the road, which is Post Office Lane.

b) Go straight on past the stile, and take the first road left into Fortunes Field, a modern housing estate. Follow this road as it bends left. At the end of the cul-de-sac, take the footpath running right between two hedges. Cross over the next road, and turn left along the pavement leading to another footpath. Continue past a stile (left) to reach a set of metal bars. After passing the first set of bars, turn left onto a track that brings you to a road. Turn right along the road, which is Post Office Lane.

6. At a T-junction, turn right through Broad Hinton to reach The Crown pub (tel. 01793-731302). If you wish to visit **Broad Hinton Church (C)** first, cross the road and turn left near the old well. Return to Post Office Lane, and walk the length of it to reach the main road (A4361) again.

7. Cross the road with care and take the signposted bridleway ahead, which runs back up to the

Ridgeway from the right hand side of The Bell (tel. 01793-731934). Keep the hedgerow on your right and pass some farm buildings. On the hillside over to your right, you should soon be able to see the **Broad Hinton White Horse (D)**. When the hedgerow ends, keep going straight ahead on the track, broadly in the direction of the large clump of trees on the Ridgeway which is furthest to the right. Go through a metal gate and keep walking uphill to reach another metal gate. Once through this, continue until you reach a T-junction with the Ridgeway. Go through one more gate to reach the Ridgeway track, and turn right.

8. Retrace your steps to the car park at Hackpen Hill.

Notes:

A: **The Science Museum at Wroughton** stores more than 22,000 objects from hovercrafts and a Lockheed Constellation airliner to examples of early computers and MRI scanners. Apart from occasional open days it is closed to the public. For more information visit sciencemuseum.org.uk or phone 01793-846200.

B: **Barbury Castle:** Around this iron age hill fort the Battle of Beran Byrig was fought in A.C. 556 as the Saxons' campaign to conquer the Romano-British pushed south. Lying within the Wessex Downs Area of Outstanding Natural Beauty, the fort and surrounding landscape became a country park in

1971 and was designated a Local Nature Reserve in 2004. In 1991, a racecourse was created nearby for point-to-point meetings.

C: **St Peter ad Vincula:** The church is one of only about 11 in England to be dedicated to this particular saint – the name means St Peter In Chains. A church has stood on this site since Saxon times, although the present building dates from the 13th century. The church contains some remarkable tombs and memorials – look out for the "handless" family of Sir Thomas Wroughton a 16th century Sheriff of Wiltshire. The Rev. Vere Awdry, vicar of Broad Hinton from 1891-95, had a son called Wilbert who also took the cloth but is best known as the author of the Thomas the Tank Engine stories. See the notes accompanying Walk 18 Box Hill for more on the Rev. Wilbert Awdry.

D: **Broad Hinton White Horse:** Sometimes known as the Hackpen Hill horse, this figure was carved to commemorate the coronation of Queen Victoria in 1837. Henry Eatwell, parish clerk for 40 years, and Robert Witt of the Crown Inn carried out the work. The carving, measuring 90 foot square, has a near neighbour – the Broad Town White Horse, about 3 miles north. Distinguished former residents of Broad Town include the late poet and critic Geoffrey Grigson (1905-1985), his wife Jane Grigson (1928-90) the cookery writer, and the great architectural historian Sir Nikolaus Pevsner (1902-

83). For further information about the Ridgeway, see the Walk 15 Silbury Hill notes.

Broad Hinton White Horse near the Ridgeway

22. EDGEWORTH

Distance:	8 miles
Time:	4 hours
Pub:	The Daneway Inn and The Bell, Sapperton
Map:	OS Explorer 168: Stroud, Tetbury & Malmesbury
Star-rating:	*** More challenging
Start/End:	Sapperton near Church entrance SO 948033

A tremendous walk through a wooded river valley from Sapperton via Pinbury Park to Edgeworth, one of the most remote Cotswold villages. The return leg passes the route of the former Thames and Severn Canal, and the Daneway Inn, a fine pub with a good-sized garden in a beautiful location. Parking is available near Sapperton Church or in the centre of the village. Sapperton lies about 13 miles north west of Malmesbury, off the A419 Cirencester-Stroud road.

Route:

From the road junction near Sapperton church, take the bridleway signposted just behind the phone box. Follow the path to enter woodland and soon emerge into a sloping grassy glade. Cut across the glade keeping to the higher ground, with the woods on your right.

Walk 22: Edgeworth

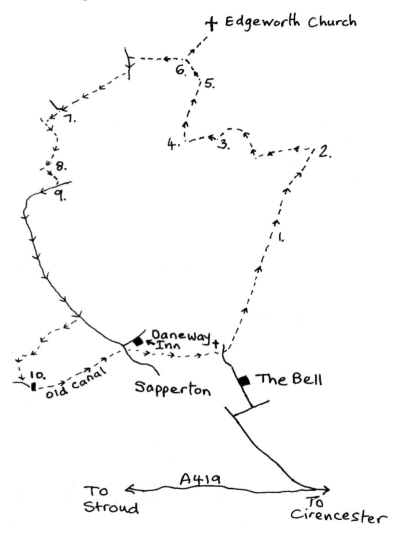

1. Follow the track downhill through trees to pass through a wide wooden gate into the undulating landscape of **Pinbury Park (A)**. Continue straight across the field, slightly to the right of the large house in the distance ahead. The path bends gently round to the right between two telegraph poles, following the contours of the hillside. Pass to the right of a large pond.

2. Turn left onto a metalled drive and stay on it past all the buildings on your right. Soon the route bends right and downhill to cross a stream via a wooden footbridge. Bear left to pass between two post and rail fences, and go through a wooden gate ahead into woodland. After about 500 yards of steady ascent on the track, go through a wide metal gate into a field.

3. Continue uphill keeping a metal fence on your right. At the corner of the field, go through another metal gate, and a third gate at the brow of the hill.

4. Turn right at this junction of paths, go through a wooden gate and continue straight ahead, keeping a stone wall on the right. Carry on in the same direction through this field and the next. Soon you see a sweep of parkland over to the right and **Edgeworth Manor** perched on the hillside ahead.

5. After passing through two wooden gates, walk downhill through parkland, keeping a metal fence on your left for about 100 yards. Aim for the house

Cattle near Sapperton

St Mary's Church, Edgeworth

on the left in the group ahead of you, as the path descends more steeply. On approaching the house, follow the path as it bends right to reach a gate. Pass through the gate to join a metalled track, which takes you to **Edgeworth (B)**. Retrace your steps back to the gate near houses.

6. Instead of taking the footpath left, back the way you came from Sapperton, take the path going right uphill to meet a track. Carry on in the same direction to meet a minor road. Turn left onto the road, then shortly right, opposite the entrance to some buildings.

7. Where the lane bends sharply to the right take the footpath left into a field. Go down the hill, keeping a metal fence on the left soon to join another path going left to right in front of you, just before a line of electricity poles. Turn left onto this path to go over a low wooden fence. Continue downhill to another stile at the far right bottom corner. Go over the stile and carry on downhill, over a tiny wooden footbridge and turn right to enter another field via a stile by a telegraph pole.

8. Bear left to continue downhill and stay close to the fence and hedge line on your left. Go through a gap in the hedge line and carry on for about 200 yards keeping a boundary on the left. Then turn sharp right past a tree and aim for the metal gate high on the other side of the valley.

9. Go through this and turn right onto a lane. At a T-junction cross the road, turn left and continue walking along the road for about ½ mile, passing three footpath signs on the right. Go right at the fourth footpath sign (where a sign for Spring Bank House is attached to a tree trunk). After about 20 yards go through the wooden gate on the left, behind which is a Gloucestershire Wildlife Trust sign. Stay on this path around the bottom of a hill on your left.

10. On reaching a T-junction of tracks turn left onto a wide path. After about 100 yards, go right over a stone bridge, then immediately left to follow the route of the former **Thames and Severn Canal (C)** through **Siccaridge Wood Nature Reserve (D)**. Continue on the path between the canal bed (left) and the River Frome (right). At a junction of paths near a wooden footbridge, turn left onto the footbridge to pass over an old lock. Then turn right onto a path running along the other side of the canal. You emerge onto a road by the Daneway Inn (tel. 01285-760297), originally built to house workers constructing the waterway. Go over the road bridge, and pick up the path on the left marked **Wysis Way (E)**. Soon you pass the Daneway portal of the Sapperton Tunnel, and the path takes you over the top of this into a field. Follow this path uphill to a kissing gate to return to Sapperton. The Bell (tel. 01285-760298) is uphill from the church.

Daneway Inn sign

Notes:

A: **Pinbury Park:** The manor was reputedly built on the site of the royal residence of Penda, the 7th century King of Mercia. After the Norman Conquest, the manor was given to the Abbess of Caen. In the 1890s, the Arts and Crafts architect Ernest Barnsley, his brother Sidney and their business partner Ernest Gimson moved in. Together they had a huge influence on the surrounding area, designing, renovating and furnishing houses – notably nearby Rodmarton Manor. Poet Laureate John Masefield lived at Pinbury Park from 1933-40.

B: **Edgeworth:** The manor was built in about 1700, although the church of St Mary next to it is of Saxon origin. Stunning views of the valley can be had from the end of the churchyard. The publisher, philanthropist and Labour peer Lord Hamlyn of Edgeworth (1926-2001) had a home in the village – one of four he owned in England and France. He was ennobled in 1998 for his patronage of the arts and the underprivileged via his charitable trust, the Paul Hamlyn Foundation, now one of the UK's largest grant-giving organisations.

C: **Thames and Severn Canal:** see Walk 6 Sapperton Tunnel notes.

D: **Siccaridge Wood Nature Reserve:** Managed by the Gloucestershire Wildlife Trust, this magical area of ancient coppice woodland and wetlands provide habitats for numerous species including the common dormouse, water shrew, wagtail, dipper and the otter.

E: **Wysis Way:** This 55-mile route was created to link Offa's Dyke with the source of the Thames near Coates, a few miles away from here, via the Forest of Dean and the Severn Vale.

23. BRINKWORTH

Distance:	4 miles
Time:	1¾ hours
Pubs:	Three Crowns, and Suffolk Arms, Brinkworth
Map:	OS Explorer 169: Cirencester & Swindon
Star-rating:	** Moderate
Start/End:	Recycling area/bus stop on the B4042 at Brinkworth SU 014844

This ramble through the countryside around England's longest village brings fine views across Dauntsey Vale. You walk alongside, under and over the Swindon to Cardiff railway and back over Ramps Hill, from which Malmesbury Abbey is often visible. Starts and finishes in Brinkworth, 5 miles east of Malmesbury on the B4042 Swindon road and on the 31 Andybus route.

Route:

From the recycling area and bus stop just beyond the Three Crowns (tel. 01666-510366) **Brinkworth (A)** go over the stile into a field and follow the left hand field edge round the back of the village hall to reach another stile round the next corner.

1. Go over the stile and go straight ahead past the rear boundary of a house. Carry on in the same direction downhill keeping a hedge on your left. Continue

over a pair of stiles into the next field and head diagonally right across it downhill in the direction of the **railway line (B)**. Go over a stile at the bottom right corner, and turn left

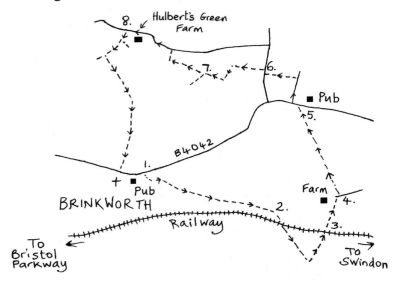

keeping the railway line on your right. Cross another two stiles, and the track beyond it. Continue in the same direction keeping parallel with the railway line. Go through a gap and straight across the field. In the far right corner, cross into the next field via a pair of stiles linked by a footbridge over a ditch. Turn left and aim for the metal gate in the middle of the field boundary ahead. Go through the gate and diagonally right across the field to a wooden gate.

2. Go through the gate (or over the stile next to it) and walk under the railway. Bear left across the next field towards a gate (note the two pill boxes behind you) and go through the gate. Turn right keeping a field edge, and soon a stream, on your right (Grittenham Brook) to the corner of the field. Don't go over the stile ahead. Instead, turn left uphill keeping a hedge and a fence on your right. Turn left again at the next corner (ignore the gate on your right) soon to reach a gate at the top of the field.

Footpath under the railway, east of Brinkworth

3. Once through the gate, turn left onto a bridge over the railway line onto a track. A few yards after the bridge, take the footpath (right) running parallel to

171

the track towards farm buildings. Rejoin the track via a stile and on reaching the farmyard turn right.

4. After a few yards, turn left onto another track opposite the entrance to a large house. Keep going in the same direction all the way to the top of the hill. Just before the back gardens of some houses, turn right through a gate, and left to reach the main road (B4042) via another gate. The Suffolk Arms (tel. 01666-510436) is a few yards to the right on the other side of the road.

5. Turn left along the grass verge adjoining the main road, then cross the road to join Bellamys Lane opposite. Continue along the lane down the hill until you see a bridleway signed left just beyond a 30 mph sign. Turn left onto the bridleway and continue past the back of some houses, keeping a hedge on the left.

6. On reaching a road, cross over, turn right and soon go left to continue on the bridleway which soon bends round to the left towards a red brick-built house. Turn right by the house and follow the track downhill.

7. Ignore the first track bending left and continue downhill. After a house on the right, but before another on your left, turn right through a parking area and go through a metal gate leading to a footbridge over a stream. After crossing over the stream, carry on in the same direction, keeping a

hedge on your left and head towards a metal kissing gate into the next field. Bear diagonally right across this into the next field and then go over a stile beside a wide wooden gate. Turn right – soon to emerge onto a lane. Turn left onto a grass verge and continue alongside the lane, sloping gently uphill, for about ½ mile.

8. After passing Hulbert's Green Farm, go through a metal gate on the left onto a bridleway. Keep a hedge on your left as you walk downhill. Ignore the first stile (left) but where the ground becomes level – about two thirds of the way down the field – cross the pair of stiles on the left. Bear right for 80 yards or so to cross a stile set in a hedge, and then keep going with a hedge on your left down to a stile at the far left corner of the field. Keep going through this field and then into the next to begin your ascent of Ramps Hill. Just before reaching the stile near the top of the hill, you may be able to see Malmesbury Abbey and the spire of St Paul's bell tower on the western horizon. Cross the stile to emerge near the top of Ramps Hill. Stay on the path around the right side of the hill, keeping a field boundary on your right, and the tower of Brinkworth church in your sights ahead. Follow the path downhill over a track and into a field. Continue straight and past the right side of the end house ahead to reach the main road (B4042) near the church. Turn left to return to the recycling area and bus stop.

View south towards Brinkworth from Ramps Hill

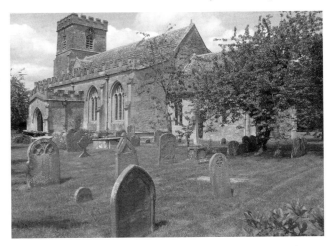

St Michael & All Angels Church, Brinkworth

Notes:

A: **Brinkworth** is England's longest village stretching 4¾ miles long east to west and almost that distance north to south – from the hamlets of Braydon to Tockenham Wick. In 2006, new road signs were erected to mark Brinkworth's claim to fame. From the churchyard of St Michael's and All Angels, on the eastern side of the Three Crowns, there are spectacular views over the Vale of Dauntsey, and the skyline towards Bristol and the Severn estuary. St Michael is said to be patron saint of the airborne, and is associated with all high places.

B: **The Swindon to Cardiff railway** running via Bristol Parkway (originally Bristol Patchway) is sometimes also known as the Badminton line. It strikes off Isambard Kingdom Brunel's original GWR (London to Bristol Temple Meads) mainline just west of Wootton Bassett passing south of Brinkworth, Little Somerford and Rodbourne and then north of Hullavington and Acton Turville.

24. NORTON & HULLAVINGTON

Distance:	6½ miles
Time:	3½ hours
Pubs:	Radnor Arms, Corston, Vine Tree, Norton, Star Inn, Hullavington
Map:	OS Explorer 168: Stroud, Malmesbury & Tetbury
Star-rating:	*** More challenging
Start/End:	Post Office and Stores, Hullavington ST 895821

Binoculars are recommended on this walk as you may spot deer, buzzards and other wildlife around the open countryside between Corston, Hullavington and Norton. Starts and finishes in Hullavington, about 4 miles south east of Malmesbury off the A429 Chippenham to Cirencester road. A number 92 bus runs between Malmesbury and Hullavington Monday to Saturday. If driving, park near the post office and stores off the main road (The Street) in Hullavington village.

Route:

With the post office and stores behind you, turn right along The Street, Hullavington, soon to pass the primary school on your left, and the cemetery on your right. On reaching a crossroads, go straight ahead on a no through road for ¼ mile towards Court Farm soon to pass under a railway line

(Swindon to Cardiff via Bristol Parkway, the old Badminton line). Continue under the railway bridge along the track for about another 400 yards, via a ford (or footbridge to the left). After about another ½ mile enter a field at the end of the track.

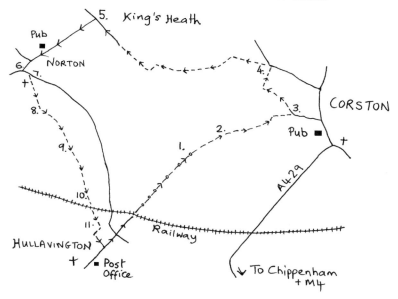

1. Go on in the same direction following the path straight across the field in front of you, alongside a row of oaks. Go through an opening in the hedge. Continue along the left edge of the field to reach a gate by an oak tree.

2. Go through the gate, turn right and keep a field boundary on your right. Soon go through a gateway into the next field, keeping Gauze Brook on your left. Cross the brook via a stone footbridge. Turn right and follow the path up to a wooden gate onto Mill Lane, Corston. To visit the Radnor Arms (tel. 01666-823389) go right from here and then right again on reaching the main road (A429). Then return to this spot, continue along Mill Lane and follow the instructions from step 3 below.

On the way to Corston

3. Turn left along Mill Lane and after West Park House enter parkland with woodland (West Park Wood) over to your left. Carry on up the hill, past a

line of trees and a private drive on your right. Immediately after this drive, take the first footpath signposted to your right via a gate. Follow this path over a stile on your right into a field, then keep a hedge on your right, to reach a lane (Common Road).

4. Turn left onto Common Road. After about 50 yards, where the road bends right, go straight ahead to join a signposted byway soon to pass a farm on your left. The large tract of open flat land you see to your right and ahead is **King's Heath (A)**. A few hundred yards past the farm, ignore the track on your right going across King's Heath. Carry straight on for about ¾ mile until you meet woodland straight ahead of you. Here, turn right along a track for about ¾ mile past farm buildings on the left.

5. At a road junction, turn left along the road or the grass verges to the village of Norton and the Vine Tree pub (tel. 01666-837654) on your right.

6. Follow the road as it bends left. Use the footbridge by the ford and continue uphill to the T-junction you can see ahead. Turn left at the T-junction. (To see **Norton Church (B)** turn right after a few paces into a no through road.) Continue along the road downhill and immediately after crossing the road bridge over the stream you will find a stile into a field on the right.

The Vine Tree, Norton

7. Climb over the stile, and then walk diagonally uphill to the opposite corner of the field. Here you will find a stile to the right of a gateway in the hedge.

8. Go over the stile and turn left following the left field edge. Go over the next stile and footbridge at the end of this field.

9. Go straight ahead through the next field, aiming for the middle of three trees ahead to join a track. Continue in the same direction soon to walk through a wide gap in the hedgerow to meet the end of a hedge ahead of you. Go straight on keeping this hedge on your left. Continue to a ditch and a stile at the far left corner of the field and carry on straight ahead.

Where the track bears round to the left, go straight ahead. Keep to the right of a hedge on your left. Cross a ditch and another stile and carry straight ahead, with the hedge still on your left. You may see the railway line (or hear a train) over to your right. Go over another stile and past the back of a large property **Bradfield Manor** (**C**) and a yew hedge.

10.　Go through a gap to your left and turn right before a concreted area in front of a barn. Continue towards a gate keeping a line of conifers on your right and a stone wall on your left. Pass under the railway line and turn left downhill. Cross a wooden footbridge then go left uphill past a sewage treatment works. Walk straight across the field aiming centre right and going to the left of an electricity pole. Then aim for the next electricity pole at the corner of a hedge and walk downhill a few paces, with the hedge on your left, to cross a small stream and a stile. Bear sharp right towards a large tree, below cottages and exit the field via a stile.

11.　Turn next right before reaching the cottages following their rear boundaries to an opening near a corner of the field. Go left through the opening and then straight ahead into a road called Newtown, which then joins the main road through Hullavington. Turn right here to visit the Star Inn (tel. 01666-837535), and return to your car or bus stop.

Notes:

A: **King's Heath:** see the notes accompanying Walk 2 Corston.

B: **All Saints, Norton:** "Humble with a presumptuous bell-turret" was Pevsner's verdict of this church, in a beautiful spot, next to the walled garden opposite Norton Manor.

C: **Bradfield Manor** is one of the few surviving great halls of the 15th century. According to the antiquarian writer John Aubrey, Bradfield was a distinct parish with its own chapel in medieval times. William Collingbourne, owner of the manor in the late 15th century was executed in 1485 for conspiring against Richard III and plotting to have Henry Tudor, the Earl of Richmond, installed on the Throne in his place. In November 2004, ex-Tory MP Neil Hamilton and his wife Christine bought Bradfield Manor.

25. BROKENBOROUGH

Distance:	5 miles
Pub:	Rose and Crown, Brokenborough
Time:	2½ hours
Map:	OS Explorer 168: Stroud, Tetbury & Malmesbury
Star-rating:	** Moderate
Start/End:	Market Cross, Malmesbury ST 934873

A relaxing walk from Malmesbury to Brokenborough and beyond past the meandering Avon (Tetbury branch) across farmland and along a section of the Fosse Way. You pass the site of a former abattoir where two Tamworth pigs made a famous escape and have the chance to visit the excellent pub at Brokenborough before returning to Malmesbury via Back Bridge.

Route:

From the Market Cross, Malmesbury, go along Birdcage Walk between a newsagent's shop and the Abbey grounds, turn right into Gloucester Street and continue past the Old Bell soon to reach the War Memorial. Cross the road to pass the memorial and continue in the same direction along Katifer Lane, next to the Three Cups (on your right).

1. At a T-junction, turn right along West Street, then bear left across Horsefair and go left again along Burnham Road. Follow this as it bends right

downhill and go straight ahead at a crossroads at the bottom of the hill to join Park Road. On the site of the new housing estate you now see on your left was the town's abattoir until the late 1990s.

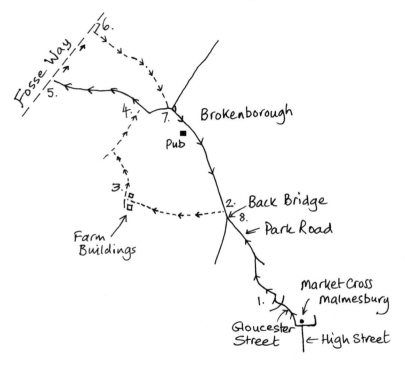

There began the tale of the **Tamworth Two (A)**. Keep going to reach a T-junction next to the **Tetbury Avon (B)**. Turn right over the river bridge (Back Bridge). After about 60 yards join the footpath signposted left into a field and pass a barn on your right.

2. Continue straight across the field to go through a gate next to a stile a few feet to the right of the river. After walking alongside the river a few yards, turn left through a gate into another field, keeping the river on your left and a hedge on your right soon to reach a farm gate. Go through the gate, and across the farmyard then turn right onto a bridleway.

Heading for Back Bridge along Park Road next to the Avon

3. Go straight on keeping a hedge and higher ground on your left. Go through a gate ahead. Bear left then follow the path right uphill. On reaching a T-junction, turn right.

4. At the next T-junction, turn left onto a lane to complete the full version of the walk (otherwise follow the ***optional short cut** after step 8). Continue along the lane for about ½ mile to reach a T-junction with a track – part of the **Fosse Way (C)**.

5. Turn right onto the Fosse Way and carry on for about a ¼ mile until you meet the River Avon and a stone footbridge to the left of it.

6. Turn right just before the river and pass to the left of a metal gate into a field. Go straight on, keeping the river on your left, and aim for a gap in the tree and hedge line ahead. Turn right towards a wide metal gate at the bottom of the hill. After passing through the gate turn immediately left uphill and left again at a corner. Once past an area of scrub on your right the ground becomes level. About 100 yards after the scrub you reach the end of a grassy track. Turn right onto the track and pass between two large cultivated areas soon to meet a hedge in front of you. Pass to the left of the hedge, and keep going in the same direction. At the other end of the hedge, go left along a track, keeping another hedge on the right. As the track starts to bend left, cross the stile on the right just beyond a wooden hand rail. Walk downhill through a field towards the right hand side of a house in the valley. Half way down the hill, bear right towards a footbridge over the Tetbury Avon into Brokenborough. Go up some steps after crossing the bridge to join a lane. Turn left.

Trish, Marion & dogs by the Avon at Brokenborough

*View north west towards Tetbury from
Brokenborough churchyard*

7.   Where the road forks, go past a yellow grit store and
then right onto the main road through the village.

Pass the church on your right. The Rose and Crown pub (tel. 01666-822302) is about 250 yards further on to your right. Continue in the same direction after the pub soon to reach Back Bridge.

8. Turn left into Park Road and return to Malmesbury centre the way you came.

*Optional short cut:

Turn right at the T-junction, and on reaching the river, take the footbridge to the right of the river bridge. Follow the path up to the church and turn right at a T-junction. You will soon see the Rose & Crown on your right. Continue in the same direction down the road and turn left into Park Road after crossing Back Bridge. Return to Malmesbury the way you came.

Notes:

A: **The Tamworth Two:** Also known as Butch and Sundance, these two pigs saved their own bacon and became international celebrities in January 1998. They broke out of the abattoir, swam across the river opposite and spent nearly two weeks on the run, with television crews and cameras in hot pursuit. After their re-capture, and a spell at an animal sanctuary near Chippenham, they were re-homed at a rare breeds farm.

B: **Tetbury Avon:** Sometimes known as the Bristol Avon, the Wiltshire Avon has two sources, one near

Tetbury the other near Sherston. The two branches meet east of Baskerville, Malmesbury. The river then winds its way to Avonmouth and the Bristol Channel via Great Somerford, Christian Malford, Chippenham, Reybridge, Melksham, Bradford-on-Avon and Bath.

C: **Fosse Way:** see the notes accompanying Walk 10 Easton Grey.

BIBLIOGRAPHY

Ashton Keynes, Somerford Keynes
The Joyful Community - Benjamin Zablocki
(Penguin Books, 1971)
Work on the Wild Side - Christopher Middleton
(Daily Telegraph, 6/11/2004)

Avebury & Silbury Hill
A Zest for Life: The story of Alexander Keiller -
Lynda J. Murray (Morven Books, 1999)

Avening & Gatcombe Park
Michael Powell - James Howard (Batsford Film
Books, 1996)
*The Buildings of England: Gloucestershire 1: The
Cotswolds* - David Verey and Alan Brooks
(Penguin, 1999)

Box Hill
Isambard Kingdom Brunel - Adrian Vaughan (John
Murray, 1991)
The Thomas the Tank Engine Man - Brian Sibley
(Heinemann, 1995)

Cerney Wick, Sapperton Tunnel & Lacock
The Wilts and Berks Canal - L.J. Dalby (The
Oakwood Press, 2000)
The Thames and Severn Canal - Humphrey
Household (Alan Sutton and Gloucestershire
County Library, 1987)

Easton Grey

Almost A Fairy Story: A History of Easton Grey House - Peter Saunders

Edgeworth

The Cotswold Village Trail - Nigel Bailey (Reardon Publishing, 1998)

Lea and Little Somerford

The Naked Gardeners - Ian and Barbara Pollard (Papdakis, 2006)
The Malmesbury Branch - Mike Fenton (Wild Swan Publications, 1990)
Ecko's of Cowbridge - Bob Browning (Cowbridge Publishing, 2005)

Luckington

The Secret Servant: The Life of Sir Stewart Menzies: Churchill's Spymaster - Anthony Cave Brown (Michael Joseph, 1988)

Shipton Moyne

Shrinking fortune forces owner to sell ancient estate - (The Times, 24 October 1996).
Selkirk's Island - Diana Souhami (Phoenix, 2002)

Westonbirt

Highgrove: Portrait of an Estate - HRH the Prince of Wales and Charles Clover (Phoenix Illustrated, 1993)

Walks Summary

	Walk	(Miles)	Star Rating
1.	Lea	3½	*
2.	Corston	6	**
3.	Malmesbury	3	*
4.	Castle Combe	5	**
5.	Luckington	4	*
6.	Sapperton Tunnel	3	*
7.	Long Newnton	3	*
8.	Shipton Moyne	4	*
9.	Cerney Wick	6	**
10.	Easton Grey	5	**
11.	Westonbirt	7½	***
12.	Lacock	6	**
13.	Little Somerford	6	**
14.	Avebury	4	*
15.	Silbury Hill	5	**
16.	Ashton Keynes	6	**
17.	Avening	6	**
18.	Box Hill	4	**
19.	Ewen	5	*
20.	Gatcombe Park	3	**
21.	Barbury Castle	7½	***
22.	Edgeworth	8	***
23.	Brinkworth	4	**
24.	Norton & Hullavington	6½	***
25.	Brokenborough	5	**

Key: * Easy   ** Moderate   *** More challenging

About the Author

The author and her dog Fly

Judy Jones began to research the first edition of this book in 2001, inspired by the long search for her lost dog around the countryside between Malmesbury and Westonbirt.

Her previous books include *Isambard's Kingdom*, *Downshifting* and *Bike Rides around Malmesbury and North Wiltshire*. She is a freelance writer and lives in Malmesbury.

If you have any comments or queries about her books then please contact her at judyjones@serneus.fsnet.co.uk